The Microsoft® Guide to

MANAGING MEMORY

with

MS-DOS® 6

The Microsoft® Guide to

MANAGING MEMORY

with

MS-DOS® 6

Installing, Configuring, and

Optimizing Memory for MS-DOS

and Windows™ Operating Systems

Microsoft
P R E S S

DAN GOOKIN

PUBLISHED BY
Microsoft Press
A Division of Microsoft Corporation
One Microsoft Way
Redmond, Washington 98052-6399

Library of Congress Cataloging-in-Publication Data
Gookin, Dan.
    The Microsoft guide to managing memory with MS-DOS 6 / Dan Gookin. -- 2nd ed.
       p. cm.
    Includes index.
    ISBN 1-55615-545-X
    1. Memory management (Computer science)   2. MS-DOS (Computer file)
I. Title.
QA76.9.M45G67   1993
004.5'3--dc20   92-44332
                                           CIP

Printed and bound in the United States of America.

1 2 3 4 5 6 7 8 9 AG-M 8 7 6 5 4 3

Distributed to the book trade in Canada by Macmillan of Canada, a division of Canada Publishing Corporation.

Distributed to the book trade outside the United States and Canada by Penguin Books Ltd.

Penguin Books Ltd., Harmondsworth, Middlesex, England
Penguin Books Australia Ltd., Ringwood, Victoria, Australia
Penguin Books N.Z. Ltd., 182-190 Wairau Road, Auckland 10, New Zealand

British Cataloging-in-Publication Data available.

Acquisitions Editor: Mike Halvorson
Project Editor: Tara Powers-Hausmann
Technical Editor: Jim Fuchs

Contents

303403

Acknowledgments

Whether trekking through the slug-infested forests of the nature trail, kneeling reverently at the globe before entering Building 16, or getting another *Not enough memory to complete the operation. OK?* message from WinWord, this project was certainly an adventure.

I'd like to thank Mike Halvorson, subtle acquisitions editor, who never pressured me to finish (even when the beta lacked MemMaker and the Mem command kept displaying negative numbers); JoAnne Woodcock, the Goddess Emeritus of DOS; Jim Brown, owner of the coveted yet miniscule corner office; Tara Powers-Hausmann, project editor; and Jim Fuchs, technical editor.

Special thanks also go to Bill Brown of Qualitas; Charles McHenry of Quarterdeck; Matt Wagner of Waterside Productions, whose other line only rings when I call; and to Sandy for letting me sneak out occasionally for a café mocha and a pink cookie.

(FREEDOM! FREEDOM! Can't you just smell all that extra RAM?)

Introduction

Memory management is a subject that has been avoided for way too long. Now the memory issue has exploded, and everyone is scrambling for cover. A few years ago there was only *expanded memory*. Then came *extended memory*. It was an $800 answer in Double Jeopardy: Which is which? Yet nagging questions still loomed: *What can I do with that memory? What makes it useful?*

Since the introduction of MS-DOS 5, the first version of the operating system to address the issue of memory management, people who have long been avoiding the subject are staring it in the face. *How can I use all that extra memory in my computer? And what can MS-DOS do with that memory?*

Now MS-DOS 6 offers even more memory-management abilities. Thanks to the handy MemMaker utility, setting up and configuring your PC's memory is a cinch. But there are still important issues, concepts, and buzzwords that will dog you to no end.

Although MS-DOS doesn't perform memory management automatically, it does assume you know what you want; MS-DOS gives you options and lets you make choices based on your personal needs. Accordingly, no one-paragraph memory solution will work for everyone. But new commands exist that can be exploited.

Consider this command:

```
dos=high
```

That one line in your CONFIG.SYS file can help free up some 50 KB of your main memory.

MS-DOS has other tricks:

- The HIMEM.SYS device driver allows MS-DOS to access an extra 64-KB region of memory and opens the door to megabytes of extra memory.

- The Devicehigh and Loadhigh commands move device drivers and memory-resident programs out of main memory, giving you more memory for your spreadsheet, network, or Microsoft Windows–based applications.

- Third-party memory managers can be used with MS-DOS to make even more memory available. The following is part of the output of the MS-DOS Mem command on a computer that is using a third-party memory manager:

```
Largest executable program size      742K  (759808 bytes)
```

IS THIS BOOK FOR YOU?

This book was written to help you get the most from MS-DOS 6 and your computer's memory. It answers the following questions:

- Exactly how is memory used in your computer?
- How can you add memory to your computer?
- How can you take advantage of all that memory?
- What can MS-DOS do to optimize memory usage?
- What are UMBs, and how do they increase available memory?
- What are the XMS and EMS standards?
- Where exactly is the HMA?
- How does Windows fit into the picture?

In addition, this book describes memory hardware—getting the most from your computer by using a RAM disk or a disk cache. To further illustrate how everything fits together, the final chapter contains several scenarios for adding and using memory on a variety of computers.

HOW TO USE THIS BOOK

This book requires no science degree. The only requirement is that you be somewhat familiar with MS-DOS. And you should wipe that stern look off your face. This book will clear up those dark, doubtful memory clouds over your head; you'll learn to get your full dollar's worth out of all that memory in your computer.

- Chapter 1 provides an introduction to memory and microprocessors.

- Chapter 2 describes how computers use memory. It also defines various terms for the different areas of memory in a computer.

- Chapter 3 introduces the Mem command, MS-DOS's way of telling you how much memory is available in your computer.

- Chapter 4 is about adding memory to your computer—the physical installation of memory chips or memory expansion cards.

- Chapter 5 concentrates on MS-DOS memory commands and how to use them.

- Chapter 6 divulges the secret for moving device drivers and memory-resident programs out of main memory.

- Chapter 7 tells you how a RAM disk and a disk cache can be used to speed up your computer.

- Chapter 8 describes how to get the most from Microsoft Windows under MS-DOS.

- Chapter 9 discusses MS-DOS and third-party memory managers.

- Chapter 10 contains several ''setup scenarios'' —describing different computers in different situations and showing how to optimize each computer's memory under MS-DOS.

- The appendixes provide a glossary and a command summary— handy at-a-glance references that help demystify the subject of memory management.

If this book contains a secret, it is simply this: Memory management is not a skill that's limited to the computer elite or the programming priesthood. It's time for *you* to pull up a chair to your computer, crack your knuckles, and start putting all that memory in your computer to work.

Chapter 1

What Is Memory?

Memory is the place where the microprocessor, the computer's brain, temporarily stores data while you work with it. Memory lets you store your ideas, express your creativity, and do your work. The more memory your computer has, the more it can do.

This chapter describes the memory inside your computer. It's introductory material, starting with a guided tour of your PC's inner workings, followed by a discussion of bits, bytes, and kilobytes, and a description of how memory is controlled by the various Intel and compatible microprocessors. This chapter establishes the background for how memory works in the PC.

LOOKING UNDER THE HOOD

With a sweeping motion of your arm, clean all the clutter off your computer desk. You're about to take a trip inside your computer, peeking and poking and prodding, finding out where the memory, the expansion slots, and the microprocessor are located. Don't be afraid—there's nothing forbidden inside.

Note: I know not everyone can suddenly pull the plug on his or her computer and visit Orville in maintenance to borrow a screwdriver. But if you can, go ahead and open it up! In the office, gather everyone around. Be bold.

Opening the Case

Before you open your computer, turn it off. Unplug it as well. (I speak from experience here. While I was working on a printer one day, a coworker happened to see it was unplugged. He dutifully plugged it back in while my fingers were inside. Trust me. Turn off the computer *and* unplug it.) You should also remove everything from the top of the

1

computer's main box (the *console* or *system unit*). If your keyboard attaches to the front of the console, unplug it and set it aside.

Now move to the back of the system unit and unscrew the screws that attach the cover to the console. (You might need to pull the system unit out, toward the front of your desk.) You will find from two to six screws, generally located at the corners of the system unit, at the top center, and maybe on the bottom. They'll all be the same type of screw, usually a Phillips head. (Don't unscrew any screws of a different size.)

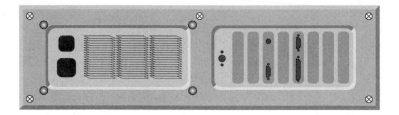

⊗   Remove these screws

◉   Do not remove these screws

After you've removed the screws, pull off the cover by sliding it toward the front of the system unit and then lifting it up at an angle. (If the cover doesn't budge, you might have forgotten a screw or the lock on the front panel.) While pulling off the cover, watch out for any ribbon cables or wires that might snag. Pull slowly enough so that you can catch these and move them out of the way. After the cover is off, set it aside.

Looking Around

Each PC is different inside, but all share similar parts. The inside of a PC contains one circuit board of electronics, usually made of green fiberglass and crawling with electronic "insects." This is the *motherboard.* Locate the motherboard at the bottom of the system unit. (See Figure 1-1.)

Look for banks of memory chips on the motherboard. They could be in a set of rows and columns of little black RAM chips called *dual in-line packages* (DIPs), or they might be standing single file on tiny cards called *single in-line memory modules* (SIMMs).

Expansion slots

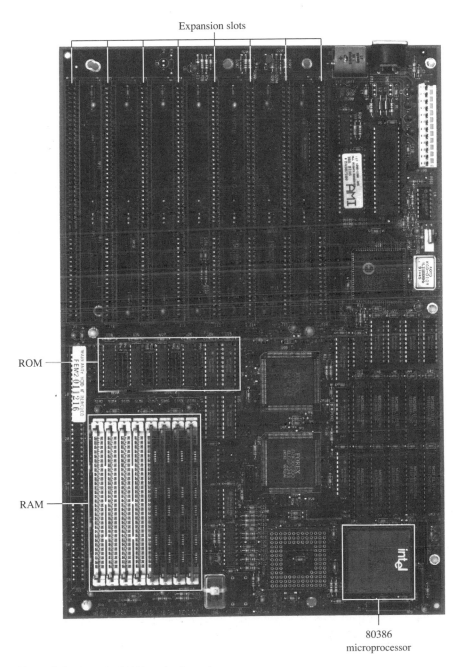

ROM

RAM

80386
microprocessor

Figure 1-1. *A typical PC motherboard.*

Some motherboards, generally those in 80386-based or i486-based computers, have special memory expansion slots. These are different from the standard expansion slots (near the back of the computer). Locate one now if you can.

Other items worth finding inside your PC are the power supply, which contains the fan and supplies power to the rest of the computer; the disk drives, both hard and floppy; the expansion slots and cards; and the computer's battery and speaker.

Look for the microprocessor. It's a flat black chip—like a Keebler Fudge Stick with small metallic legs—either rectangular or square. On top of the chip you'll see numbers such as 8088, 8086, 80286, 80386, i486, V20, V30, and so on. Gently push any wires or cables out of the way if it's crowded in there.

Note: Not every system has a visible microprocessor. For example, the microprocessor in my Dell 386 is located under the hard disk and out of sight.

Finally look toward the back of the motherboard at the rows of expansion slots. These expansion slots are connected to the computer's *bus,* a communications link between the microprocessor and other devices. Specially designed cards plug into these expansion slots. One type of card you can plug into a slot is a *memory expansion card.* After the motherboard is fully populated with memory chips, a memory expansion card allows you to add more memory to the computer.

Close 'Er Up

That wraps up the tour of your PC. To put the cover back on, position it over the front of the system unit and carefully slide it back. Keep cables out of the way so that they won't snag.

Note: If you were adding memory at this point, you wouldn't put the cover back on. Instead, it's a good idea to test the memory in the computer with the cover off. That way you can fix any problems without repeatedly removing and replacing the cover. Be sure the power is off while doing this—never insert or remove a card or a memory chip while the power is on.

Push the cover back as far as possible. If the cover doesn't go all the way back, it might be improperly aligned; be sure that the lip at the base of the computer is inside the cover. Also, check the key to be sure the computer isn't locked, and check inside to be sure the cover hasn't caught any cables. Then insert and start tightening the cover screws. When you're done, simply plug in the system unit, connect the monitor (and keyboard, if necessary), and turn on the computer.

BITS, BYTES, KILOBYTES, AND MEGABYTES

Memory is where your computer stores information. But how? How can something as lovely as a poem or as creative as an Escher illustration be stored electronically?

Computers know nothing of words, sounds, shades of gray, or perspective. What they do know is "on" and "off"—the presence or absence of electricity. *On* is equal to about 5 volts of current; *off* is equal to no current. To us, the computer represents *on* and *off* in its memory with the values 1 and 0.

You can't get too far with a 1 and a 0. These are the digits in the *binary* (base-two) system. Humans, probably because we have 10 fingers, use the *decimal* (base-ten) system, which uses digits from 0 through 9. A 0 or a 1 is known as a *binary digit,* which contracts to form the word *bit*.

A bit can store only one of two values: 0 or 1. Combining multiple bits increases the amount of information that can be stored. For example, 2 bits can store four binary numbers: 00, 01, 10, and 11. These are the decimal numbers 0, 1, 2, and 3. If you've never seen binary numbers before, this sequence might look a little strange. Why is 1 stored as 01, but 2 stored as 10?

Consider the decimal number 307. Each digit in the number is multiplied by a different power of 10: the 7 is the units digit (10 to the power of 0, which is 1—any number raised to the power of 0 is 1); the 0 is the tens digit (10 to the power of 1); and the 3 is the hundreds digit (10 to the power of 2). So the decimal number 307 is $3\times100 + 0\times10 + 7\times1$.

The binary system works the same way—only each digit is multiplied by a power of *2*. Consider the binary number 101. The digit furthest to the right is multiplied by 2 to the power of 0 (1), the next digit to the left is multiplied by 2 to the power of 1 (2), the next digit to the left is multiplied by 2 to the power of 2 (4), and so on. Therefore, the binary number 101 is 1×4 + 0×2 + 1×1, which is equal to the decimal number 5.

A *byte* is a group of 8 bits. It is the smallest collection of bits that the microprocessor can work with. This grouping allows 256 different combinations. (In general, the number of combinations possible by combining bits is 2 raised to the power of the number of bits in the group; 2 raised to the eighth power is 256.) Therefore, a byte can store a number in the range 0 through 255. The microprocessor knows the location, or *address,* of each byte in memory, and it can store or read the byte at any given address.

When you think of a byte in memory, picture it as storing one character of information. The word ''door'' requires 4 bytes of memory. A paragraph might require 400 bytes; a page of text, almost 2000 bytes. The numbers grow and grow, like dust bunnies under the couch.

As you deal with more and more memory, other terms come into play. A *kilobyte* (KB) is approximately 1000 bytes of information. (Technically, a kilobyte is 1024 bytes, but in the binary number system, 1024 is the closest power of 2 to the decimal number 1000.) A page of text takes about 2 KB of memory.

To store text, you need only a few kilobytes of memory. For example, no chapter in this book takes up more than 32 KB of memory space. (The whole book occupies only 316 KB.) But when you deal with graphics and sound, much more memory is required.

The number of bytes needed to store a graphics image is staggering. Look at a picture of a rose on your screen and ponder this: It might take 500 KB or more to store that image. A 60,000-word novel uses less storage space. So I guess it's safe to say that a picture on a computer is worth well over 1000 words!

In the early days of the personal computer, no one dreamed of storing multicolored images in a PC—there wasn't enough memory! But with newer PCs that have millions of bytes of memory, today it's possible.

A *megabyte* (MB) is approximately 1,000,000 bytes of memory. Technically, it's 1024 KB (1024 times 1024 bytes, or 1,048,576 bytes, which is 8,388,608 bits—a mind-boggling amount). But this is nothing! An 80386 microprocessor can access 4096 MB of memory, or 4 *gigabytes* (GB).

Memory storage is closely related to a computer's potential. The more memory your computer has, the more you can do with your computer (just as the more brain cells you have, the better you are at Jeopardy). More memory opens up avenues for storing more diverse information, such as spreadsheets, music, graphics, and so on. The terms *bits, bytes, kilobytes,* and *megabytes* describe the quantity of memory your computer has.

MICROPROCESSORS AND MEMORY

Memory is necessary because the microprocessor, your computer's brain, really has no place to put things. Having enough memory has always been important. You would think the more the better. But the design of the microprocessor actually limits the amount of memory it can use.

One measure of a microprocessor's power is the width of its *data bus*. This is like an electronic data highway—the wider the data bus (the more ''lanes''), the more data can be moved at the same time. A microprocessor has both an internal and an external data bus. The internal data bus moves data between the internal components of the microprocessor. The external data bus is for communication between the microprocessor and other parts of the computer, such as disk drives, expansion cards, and memory.

Another measure of a microprocessor's power is the width of its *address bus*. The width of a microprocessor's address bus determines the amount of memory it can access. For example, the 8086, which has a 20-bit address bus, can access 1 MB of memory. The 80286, with its 24-bit address bus, can access 16 MB of memory.

The term *bits* is commonly used to describe a microprocessor's data bus width. For example, the 8086 is called a 16-bit microprocessor because it has an internal 16-bit data bus. The microprocessor in the original IBM PC was an Intel 8088. The 8088 is a hybrid—it's known as an 8/16-bit microprocessor because the 8088 has an external 8-bit data bus but an internal 16-bit data bus.

True, this is funky. The 8088's sister, the 8086, has an internal and an external 16-bit data bus. But the chips required to support the 8086 cost more, so IBM went with the 8088.

Regardless of the technical differences, both the 8088 and the 8086 have a 20-bit address bus and both can access 1 MB of memory. The maximum amount of memory the microprocessor can access is referred to as its *address space*.

This history lesson is important because all PC "clones"—including the system you have on your desk right now—are based on the original PC. All these computers followed the same system design, which was limited by the 8088/8086's 1 MB of address space. Other design factors came into play, which is one reason why memory is so complicated in today's PC. (This is explained in the next chapter, "How Your Computer Uses Memory.")

Microprocessor	Bits	Megabytes
8088	8/16	1
8086	16	1
80286	16	16
80386SX	16/32	16
80386	32/32	4096
i486SX	32/32	4096
i486	32/32	4096
i486DX2	32/32	4096

The PC/AT came with an 80286 microprocessor, which is actually the grandchild of the 8086. (The 80186—Intel's next "generation" of microprocessor—was used in some computers, notably the Tandy 2000, but really offered no outstanding memory features over the 8086.) The 80286 has an internal and external 16-bit data bus. It also has a 24-bit address bus, which allows it to access 16 MB of memory.

The 80386 microprocessor—the PC's dream chip—has an internal and external 32-bit data bus. It's compatible with the 80286 and the 8086, but it has a 32-bit address bus, so it can address an astonishing 4096 MB of memory.

The best thing about the 80386 is its ability to exploit memory between 640 KB and 1 MB, an ability that MS-DOS uses to full advantage. Because of its power, the 80386—and its offspring, the i486—is quickly becoming the standard microprocessor for PC computing.

The 80386 has a little sister, the 80386SX, which has an internal 32-bit data bus and all the memory magic of the 80386. However, the 80386SX is rated as a 16/32-bit microprocessor; it has only an external 16-bit data bus. The 80386SX is cheaper than the 80386 (also called the 80386DX), which makes a PC with an 80386SX an excellent alternative to a PC with an 80286.

The current rage among PC microprocessors is the i486 (including the i486SX and the i486DX2). Although this has 32-bit data and address buses, it offers some extra power and features over the 80386. For the purposes of memory, the i486 works in the same way as the 80386 and 80386SX. In this book, the term *'386* refers to any PC with an 80386SX, 80386, i486SX, i486, i486DX2, or the Pentium microprocessor.

Note: The next-generation microprocessor after the i486 is the Pentium. *This might be referred to as the 586, though for copyright purposes, Intel chose to name it Pentium. The Pentium is compatible with the 80386 and i486 chips. Therefore, the Pentium and any chips compatible with it fall into the '386 "family" discussed in this book.*

The purpose of this history lesson is to make you familiar with how a microprocessor's power is related to the amount of memory it can use. The problem is that MS-DOS was written for the 8088 with its paltry 1-MB address space. Earlier versions of MS-DOS treated a '386 like a fast 8088. That's not very efficient, nor does it take advantage of the full memory potential of the '386. This is why MS-DOS 6 (and version 5 before it) is different: It lets you have the memory and use it too.

HOW MEMORY WORKS

If you've always wondered how a row of flat chips and electricity can store information, the following explanation of memory should tickle your curiosity bone. All told, there are two basic types of computer memory: *RAM* and *ROM*.

The bulk of your computer's memory is *random access memory* (RAM). RAM is memory that the computer can read from and write to. RAM is *volatile* memory—whenever you shut off the computer, any information stored in RAM is lost. There are two types of RAM: *dynamic* RAMs (DRAMs) and *static* RAMs (SRAMs).

DRAMs have a large storage capacity and a low power consumption. Their memory cells are basically charge-store capacitors that you can think of as teeny tiny batteries. The presence or absence of a charge in the battery is interpreted as a logical 1 or 0. Because the batteries tend to lose their charge, DRAMs require a periodic charge-refresh cycle—an electronic shot in the arm—to maintain data storage. This "refresh cycle" slows down the operation of DRAMs.

SRAMs store 1 and 0 using a different method—a method that doesn't require refreshing. They are faster than DRAMs but have a smaller storage capacity and are expensive to manufacture. For these reasons, most if not all the RAM chips in your computer are DRAMs.

ROM stands for *read-only memory*—memory that cannot be written to or updated. ROMs are not volatile: A ROM chip retains its contents even when the power is off. Because of this, ROMs are used to store special instructions (how to load the operating system at boot time, how to control a hardware device) or other vital programming code for your computer. Unless you get into some very serious programming, these ROM instructions are completely transparent to you: The computer finds and uses them when it needs to with no intervention from you at all.

A RAM chip is rated by how many bits it can contain. There are 16-Kb (kilobit), 64-Kb, 128-Kb, 256-Kb, and 1-Mb (megabit) RAM chips. But note that these chips store individual bits, not entire bytes. Why? Because RAM chips in IBM PC and compatible computers are arranged in *banks* (rows).

Because a byte has 8 bits, a bank should have eight RAM chips. On a PC, however, a bank has a bonus ninth chip. Each chip supplies 1 of the 8 bits in the byte, and the ninth chip supplies a *parity bit.* The parity bit provides error checking on the other 8 bits, ensuring their reliability.

Note: Think of a 256-Kb RAM chip as a stack of 256,000-odd bits. In order to make 256 KB, you need eight (plus one) stacks of 256,000 bits. That's how one bank of 256-Kb RAM chips equals 256 KB of memory. The same holds true for 1-Mb chips; you need nine of them to make 1 MB of memory.

Four more terms will help you understand memory: *access time, wait state, interleaving,* and *cache memory.*

Access Time

Memory is rated for speed as well as capacity. The microprocessor is constantly writing and reading numbers to and from memory. For example, the microprocessor might want a specific number stored in memory location 100,000. It takes a certain amount of time for memory to store the number and go through a refresh cycle. This delay is known as the memory's *access time.* Access time is measured in nanoseconds (ns), or billionths of a second. The lower the access time, the faster the memory.

Wait State

Ideally, the memory is fast enough to store the number and go through a refresh cycle before the microprocessor is ready to store another number. If not, the microprocessor must wait one or more *clock cycles,* biding its time, while memory finishes refreshing. (Think of a clock cycle as an electronic "heartbeat.") Each clock cycle the microprocessor must wait while memory is being refreshed is known as a *wait state.* Zero wait states, the optimal arrangement, means that the microprocessor never has to wait for a memory refresh.

Interleaving

Memory chips are traditionally arranged in rows, with a range of memory locations within each row, as shown in Figure 1-2 on the next page. With this arrangement, DRAMs simply can't keep up with today's 33-MHz (or faster) microprocessors because of the time required for the refresh cycle.

SRAMs are fast enough, but they are very expensive. Fortunately, a memory arrangement was discovered that minimizes the slow memory/ fast microprocessor problem. This memory arrangement is known as *interleaved memory.*

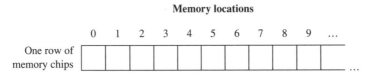

Memory locations

Figure 1-2. *Traditional memory chip arrangement.*

Typically, a program accesses memory sequentially. If a program wants to store a number in memory location 100,000, the program will probably want to store a number at memory location 100,001, then 100,002, and so on. Interleaved memory therefore divides a range of memory locations into two rows of memory chips. The first row contains even-numbered memory locations; the second row contains odd-numbered memory locations, as shown in Figure 1-3. These rows undergo memory refresh on odd and even clock cycles.

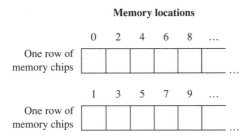

Memory locations

Figure 1-3. *Interleaved memory chip arrangement.*

Now when the microprocessor stores a number in location 100,000, location 100,001 is being refreshed. When the microprocessor stores a number at location 100,001, location 100,002 is being refreshed. This simple arrangement helps slower memory keep up with speedy microprocessors.

Cache Memory

Cache memory is a small amount (typically 8 to 256 KB) of very fast SRAM memory that sits between the microprocessor and the main memory.

When the microprocessor reads data from or stores data in main memory, that data is stored in the cache memory as well. If the microprocessor needs that data again, the microprocessor reads the data from the cache memory rather than the slower main memory. Intel incorporates 8 KB of cache memory directly into the i486 microprocessor.

Because cache memory contains SRAMs, it's expensive, sometimes adding $300 to the price of the computer. But the speed increase is dramatic. Buy a computer with cache memory if you can afford the added cost. Unlike the other kinds of memory we'll be discussing in this book, you can't add cache memory to your computer—you must purchase a system that already has cache memory installed because cache memory is an integral part of the motherboard.

Note: Be sure to check your computer's user manual before buying extra memory chips. It should list the size and speed of the chips your computer needs. It doesn't hurt to buy faster chips, but slower chips will cause unnecessary wait states and hurt all-around system performance.

None of these terms, nor any of the information in this section, is crucial to understanding how MS-DOS works with memory. If you want more information and happen to be in the Boston area, the Boston Computer Museum has an excellent display on how memory works. Visit the museum if you're ever in Beantown.

SUMMARY

Memory is the temporary storage area for your computer. The amount of memory your computer can access is directly related to its microprocessor. The more powerful the microprocessor—the wider its address bus— the more memory it can access. The drawback used to be MS-DOS, which forced device drivers, memory-resident programs, and applications programs to compete for memory space in the lower 640 KB of the 1 MB of memory accessed by the original PC's microprocessor. With MS-DOS versions 5 and later, that has changed.

■ A bit is a binary digit and has one of two values: 0 or 1.

■ Bits are grouped 8 to a byte.

■ A byte can store one of 256 values. Think of a byte as a character.

■ A kilobyte is approximately 1000 bytes (technically, 1024 bytes).

■ A megabyte (1024 KB) is approximately 1,000,000 bytes (technically, 1,048,576 bytes).

■ The 8088/8086 microprocessors have an 8-bit and a 16-bit data bus, respectively. They can directly address 1 MB of RAM.

■ The 80286 microprocessor has a 16-bit data bus and can directly address 16 MB of RAM.

■ The 80386 microprocessor has a 32-bit data bus and can directly address 4096 MB of RAM.

Chapter 2

How Your Computer Uses Memory

It's idealistic to think of a computer containing 1 MB of RAM. There's something pure and surreal about 1 MB of clean, uninterrupted memory—like that endless, grassy fairway without a tree or a sand trap. Regardless, memory inside a computer simply isn't a smooth, contiguous bank of nine RAM chips. Instead, memory is separated and classified according to the computer's needs.

This chapter is about the arrangement of memory inside the typical PC. It's also about terminology, and when it comes to understanding memory, terminology is key.

THE PC'S MEMORY

When IBM designed its first microcomputer, the PC, it used the 8088 microprocessor. The 8088 (and 8086) can access 1 MB of RAM, meaning it has an address space of 1 MB.

IBM's engineers had to assign part of that address space to the necessary ROM and the rest to RAM. They decided that the lower 640 KB would be used for RAM and that the upper 384 KB would be reserved for ROM. When the PC made its debut, it did not have a full megabyte of memory, but the line had been drawn: Below 640 KB was for RAM and for use by MS-DOS and applications; above 640 KB was reserved for use by ROM, the video adapters, and so on.

This line is where the two basic terms for describing the PC's memory come into play: *conventional memory* and *upper memory*.

■ Conventional memory is the PC's basic RAM, from 0 KB through 640 KB. Conventional memory is also referred to as *low-DOS memory*.

■ Upper memory is the memory area above 640 KB, reserved for ROM. Upper memory is also referred to as *reserved memory* or *high-DOS memory*.

Conventional Memory

Conventional memory is where MS-DOS loads and runs your programs. The lower part of conventional memory is reserved for use by the computer, but from about the 2-KB mark on up to 640 KB, you can run applications. This doesn't mean that you have the full 640 KB (or 638 KB) available for all your RAM-greedy applications. After all, MS-DOS dwells in conventional memory, eating up anywhere from 18 KB to 90 KB depending on the MS-DOS version.

Atop MS-DOS are some *data storage areas*—places MS-DOS uses to manage any open files, plus any device drivers loaded with CONFIG.SYS and any memory-resident programs that AUTOEXEC.BAT loads. Ultimately, on top of it all, is your application and any files you've loaded for use with the application, such as a document or a spreadsheet.

In the worst-case scenario, with enough device drivers and memory-resident programs loaded, you might have only a few dozen kilobytes of conventional memory left over for running your applications. But is this enough?

The Upper Memory Area

IBM reserved the upper 384 KB of the PC's memory for future expansion or for ROM. The original PC used only a sliver of that memory for its *BIOS*, the Basic Input/Output System that provided the PC with low-level instructions for controlling peripheral devices such as disk drives and the keyboard. Another small portion was used for video memory, where the information to be displayed on the monochrome or color display was stored. And yet plenty of room existed for expansion.

RAM Cram

The proliferation of memory-resident programs peaked in the mid-1980s. At that time, just about every program could make itself resident, giving you instant access to the program at the touch of a ''hot key.'' Although few programs needed to be resident, making them so was a good sales gimmick.

The problems with memory-resident (also known as *Terminate and Stay Resident*, or TSR) programs were many. First no one standardized a way to create them. Programs would conflict, each trying to wrest control of the computer. Second MS-DOS didn't help, providing no rules or regulations for the horde of memory-resident software. Finally the memory-resident programs were using large areas of conventional memory — a condition known as *RAM cram*.

Eventually, the madness ceased. Today you can still find memory-resident programs, but most are utilities. The urge to produce the ''pop-up application'' has vanished. And with the advent of multitasking environments such as Microsoft Windows, there is less need than ever for memory-resident applications.

Today, the upper memory area still hasn't filled with ROM. The first 128 KB are used for video memory (RAM): the monochrome, CGA, EGA, or VGA graphics systems in most PCs. The next 128 KB are reserved for installable ROMs such as video ROM and the hard-disk controller ROM. The last 128 KB are reserved for the ROM BIOS. Figure 2-1 on the following page shows how all this memory is allocated, using the traditional memory map.

The 640-KB MS-DOS Barrier

As programs grew in size, and as new microprocessors that could access more memory were introduced, the limitations of the original PC design became apparent. Instead of being known as the point where program RAM stops and upper memory starts, the 640 KB point became known as

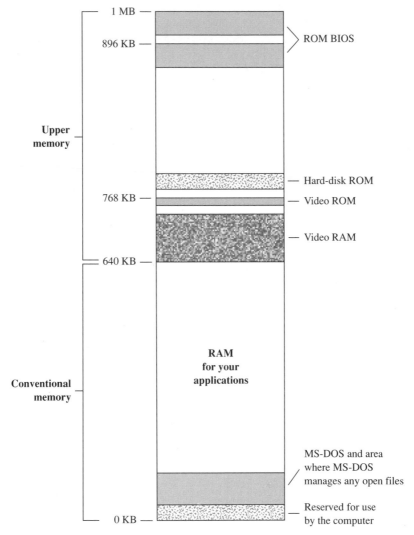

Figure 2-1. *The PC memory map.*

the *MS-DOS barrier*—a brick wall beyond which use of memory was forbidden.

Programs could work only in the 640 KB (or less) of RAM that MS-DOS gave them. In 1981, that was 10 times the amount available in any other microcomputer. But by the late 1980s, it was considered a pathetic amount of memory. Solutions were sought.

EXPANDED MEMORY

Spreadsheet users were the first to scream for more memory. While you're working on a spreadsheet, it is stored in memory; the more memory you have, the larger the spreadsheet you can generate. For the home budget, 256 KB was enough memory. For a small office, 640 KB was fine. But for Big Spreadsheet Users, 640 KB wasn't enough.

A solution was devised using a combination of both hardware and software. Lotus, Intel, and Microsoft devised the LIM Expanded Memory Specification (EMS) standard for *expanded memory*, essentially a pool of extra memory in a PC. This isn't memory beyond the 1-MB mark, nor can programs run there. Instead, it's more like a memory storage area on an EMS-compatible expansion card inside the computer. EMS-compatible software can access the memory on the card, which in turn means more memory for storing data.

To access and use expanded memory on your computer, you need both an EMS-compatible memory expansion card and a device driver known as an *expanded memory manager* (EMM). You also need EMS-compatible applications that can use the expanded memory.

How Expanded Memory Works

Expanded memory takes advantage of an unused area of upper memory, reserving one 64-KB block of memory called the *page frame*. (See Figure 2-2 on the following page.) The expanded memory sits by itself—away from the main memory in a PC—on an expansion card in one of the PC's expansion slots.

The EMM device driver makes expanded memory available to application software as four 16-KB *pages* mapped into the page frame. This memory is *bank-switched* by the hardware and software, meaning the 16-KB pages can be swapped in and out of the page frame as needed. As soon as it's in the page frame, a page can be accessed by the microprocessor because it falls within the 1-MB address space.

Using the functions provided by the EMM device driver, your applications can map other pages of expanded memory into the page frame. That's how expanded memory is used.

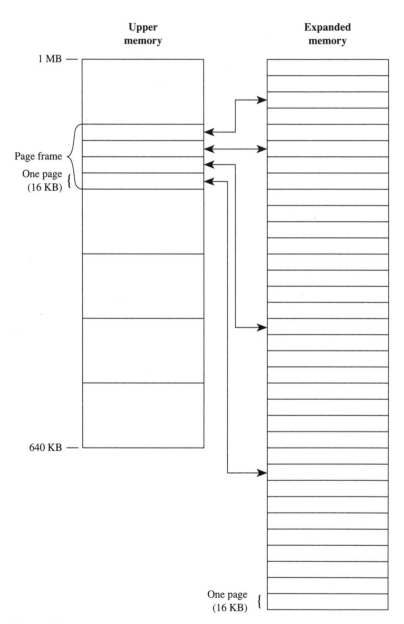

Figure 2-2. *How expanded memory is accessed.*

Note: EMS version 3.2 is really designed for storage, not for running pro-grams. Mapping 16-KB pages of expanded memory into the page frame is fine for keeping unused portions of a spreadsheet in quick reach. But actual pro-grams require contiguous memory directly accessible by the microprocessor.

The latest version of the EMS standard, version 4.0, provides access to as much as 32 MB of expanded memory. The EMS 4.0 standard allows newer EMS cards to move programs as well as data into expanded memory. As a result, expanded memory becomes more useful for multitasking, but it is still much slower than directly addressing conventional memory.

Using Backfill

In the early days, the PC came with 256 KB or less of installed memory on the motherboard. The only way to add memory was with a memory expan-sion card. With dropping memory prices, most computers today come with 1 MB or more.

An early function of the EMS expanded memory cards was to supply con-ventional memory in addition to expanded memory. The cards could be configured to give a 256-KB PC an extra 384 KB of conventional memory for a full 640 KB—and whatever memory was left over was configured as expanded memory. The process of filling in that conventional memory with expanded memory is known as *backfilling*.

If your 8088, 8086, or 80286 computer already has 640 KB of conventional memory, you might consider disabling some of that memory. (This can usually be done with switches on the motherboard.) Then let a LIM EMS 4.0 expanded memory card fill in the disabled conventional memory with expanded memory.

This creates what is known as *mappable conventional memory*. This memory is like one huge page frame: The EMM device driver can swap all the backfill memory in and out of expanded memory. LIM EMS 4.0 theoretically lets the EMM device driver swap the entire 1-MB address range of the 8086 with expanded memory.

In practice, however, most EMS 4.0 memory boards are not fully com-pliant with the EMS 4.0 standard. For example, the Intel Above Board can only backfill conventional memory in the range 256 KB through 640 KB.

Note: The '386 microprocessor has powerful memory-mapping capabilities. Although 8088/8086 and 80286 systems require LIM EMS-compatible hardware and software, the '386 can simulate expanded memory in extended memory using an expanded memory emulator. This subject is covered in detail in Chapters 5 and 9.

What Is Shadow RAM?

Shadow RAM is a technology that copies video and system BIOS into an unused area of RAM that is reassigned, or "mapped," into upper memory when the computer boots. Because RAM is faster than ROM, this enhances overall system performance. Like cache memory, shadow RAM can't be added to your computer—you must purchase a system that already has shadow RAM installed.

If you want to buy a computer with shadow RAM, be sure the shadow RAM can be disabled. Such a disable feature is important with some applications to resolve memory conflicts.

EXTENDED MEMORY

What is extended memory? Basically, extended memory is memory above and beyond the 1-MB mark on an 80286-based or '386-based PC. Remember: above and beyond. *Above* where MS-DOS resides, and *beyond* the reach of most MS-DOS applications.

The 80286 can access up to 16 MB of RAM; the '386 can access up to 4096 MB. In all of those systems, versions of MS-DOS prior to MS-DOS 5 treated the 80286 and later microprocessors as a fast 8088 microprocessor with 1 MB of memory. Any memory above that 1-MB mark is referred to as *extended memory*. Figure 2-3 shows the memory map for a typical 80286-based or '386-based computer with extended memory.

The biggest problem with extended memory is that it's above the 8088's address space—therefore, MS-DOS cannot directly use extended memory.

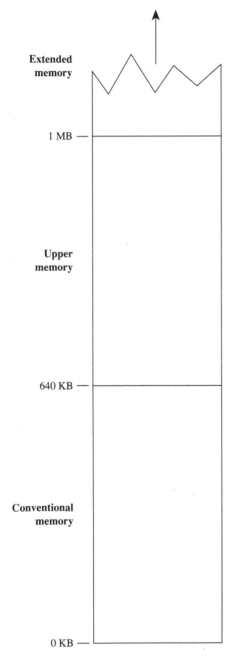

Figure 2-3. *The memory map for an 80286-based or '386-based computer with extended memory.*

To use extended memory, a program must switch the microprocessor to protected mode and then switch the microprocessor back to real mode before quitting. (See the next section in this chapter, "Real and Protected Modes.") The first programs to exploit this technique were RAM disks.

Because expanded memory was introduced before extended memory, more programs are designed to use expanded memory than extended memory. This is changing, however. AutoCAD and Lotus 1-2-3 release 3.x can use extended memory. And Microsoft Windows in enhanced mode opens the door to megabytes of extended memory.

Real and Protected Modes

To understand extended memory, you must dive into the capabilities of the 80286 and '386 microprocessors. These microprocessors actually have two modes of operation: *real mode* and *protected mode.*

- In real mode, the 80286 microprocessor operates in the same way as an 8088; it can access only 1 MB of RAM, and extended memory can't be used for running programs.

- In protected mode, the 80286 cuts loose. It can access up to 16 MB of RAM and run programs anywhere. Extended memory is wide open for the microprocessor.

A '386 has real and protected modes, just like the 80286. In real mode, a '386 operates as a very fast 8088, but in protected mode a '386 can access up to 4096 MB of RAM for running programs and storing information. Additionally, when running an operating system that supports protected mode, a '386 has a mode called *virtual 8086,* or V-86, mode. In that mode, the operating system can run multiple programs. Each program believes it is running on a separate 8088 microprocessor with its own unique 1-MB address space. This is how DESQview/386 multitasks MS-DOS applications.

Protected mode sounds like a RAM-hungry user's dream: lots of memory and the full power of the microprocessor to use it. Yet MS-DOS is linked to the 8088; it's a real-mode-only operating system. MS-DOS cannot run in protected mode, nor can it run programs in extended memory.

Using Extended Memory Under MS-DOS

Although extended memory is really out of the MS-DOS picture (for now), some potential exists:

■ Some applications can run in—and will use—extended memory. These are the so-called *extended-DOS* applications. Secretly, these programs switch the microprocessor from real to protected mode—behind MS-DOS's back. When the application runs, it takes advantage of the full power of the microprocessor and all the extended memory in the computer. When the application quits and returns to MS-DOS, the application downshifts the microprocessor back into real mode. A few programs do this, most notably Windows, Lotus 1-2-3 release 3.x, and some versions of AutoCAD.

■ Since MS DOS version 3.2, extended memory has been available for use as memory storage. You can place RAM disks, disk caches, or print buffers into extended memory. (This topic is covered in Chapter 7.) As long as programs aren't running in that memory, MS-DOS can access it for storage purposes.

■ Extended memory can be used to simulate expanded memory—but only on '386-based computers and only with the proper software (an expanded memory emulator).

In order to accomplish these feats, Lotus, Intel, AST Research, and Microsoft established a standard for dealing with extended memory under MS-DOS. It's the *Extended Memory Specification*, or XMS.

XMS doesn't allow programs to run in extended memory; you're still limited to the three functions described above. But XMS does establish the standards that provide sophisticated, cooperative use of extended memory under MS-DOS.

MS-DOS SOLUTIONS

MS-DOS 5 opened up new doors for using memory on a PC, especially 80286-based and '386-based systems. MS-DOS 6 continues the tradition, but along with the new opportunities come some new terms used to describe memory.

The High Memory Area

The 8088/8086 microprocessors can address 1 MB of memory. Any attempt to address memory above 1 MB causes the microprocessor to *wrap around*, back to memory location 0. (This works like the old Asteroids video game: When you flew your ship off the top of the screen, your ship reappeared at the bottom of the screen.)

The 80286 and '386 also wrap around to location 0. They can also map these bytes into the first 64 KB of extended memory. These extra 65,520 bytes are known as the *high memory area*, or HMA. Refer to Figure 2-4. Assume that the HMA provides MS-DOS with an extra 64 KB of memory, even though the HMA is actually 16 bytes short of 64 KB.

That extra memory can be used by MS-DOS on an 80286-based or '386-based computer. MS-DOS can actually "see" the memory sitting up there and access it directly without having to switch the microprocessor into protected mode.

To access the HMA—an extra 64 KB of memory—you need two things:

■ An 80286-based or '386-based PC with extended memory

■ A device driver to access and control the HMA

Why Not Write a Protected-Mode Version of MS-DOS?

A protected-mode version of MS-DOS once existed! It was OS/2 version 1, introduced in 1987 for the specific purpose of giving the 80286 a protected-mode operating system. OS/2 version 1 did not last long because the majority of PC users at the time were satisfied with MS-DOS and worried over the risks of switching operating systems.

Today, protected-mode operating systems for the PC abound. The most popular is Microsoft Windows, which lets you use the power of your PC without being encumbered by MS-DOS's memory limitations or RAM Cram.

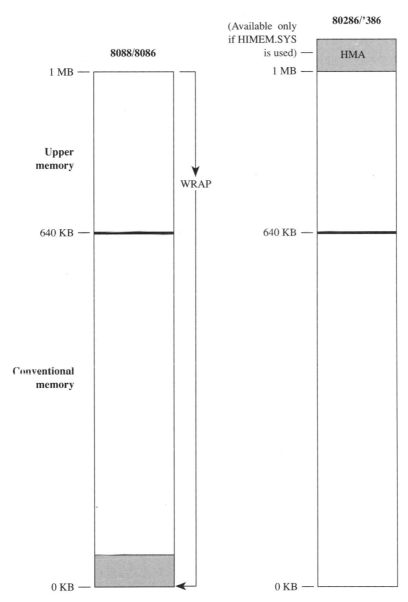

Figure 2-4. *How to fool MS-DOS into seeing an extra 64 KB of memory.*

Most 80286-based and '386-based PCs come with 1 MB of RAM installed.
The first 640 KB of that memory is conventional memory. The rest is usually extended memory. (Note that some older AT computers come with
only 512 KB of memory installed.) Therefore, nearly all 80286-based or
later computers have the extended memory needed for MS-DOS to access
the HMA.

The device driver that accesses the HMA is HIMEM.SYS. Additionally,
HIMEM.SYS implements the XMS standard on 80268-based and '386-
based computers running under MS-DOS. It's the first step toward taking
full advantage of your computer's memory potential.

Upper Memory Regions

Upper memory regions are unused areas in upper memory. See Figure 2-5.

Although IBM set aside 384 KB for ROM and future expansion, very little
of it is used. The BIOS uses only part of the upper 128 KB of this memory;
the hard-disk controller and video BIOS occupy only a sliver of the
memory; and the video memory takes up anywhere from 4 KB (for monochrome) to 32 KB (for CGA) to 128 KB (for both EGA and VGA). As a result,
there are unused portions of upper memory, or upper memory regions.

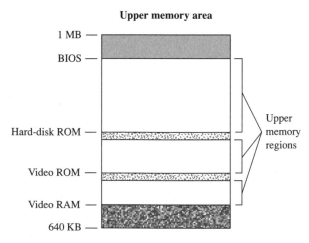

Figure 2-5. *Where upper memory blocks are created.*

The memory regions between the various ROMs and other goodies in reserved memory cannot be used to run programs. Why? Because there is no actual RAM up there. RAM stops at 640 KB. (While it's true that video RAM is in reserved memory, it's designated for the video system, not for running programs.)

Before MS-DOS 5, you needed to buy a third-party memory management program, such as 386MAX from Qualitas or QEMM-386 from Quarterdeck, if you wanted to take advantage of the unused upper memory regions. Those programs would map expanded memory into the unused upper memory regions between 640 KB and 1 MB to create upper memory blocks, or *UMBs*.

Starting with version 5, MS-DOS now includes the necessary device drivers and programs needed to create UMBs in usable regions of upper memory on any '386-based computer that has extended memory. The UMBs can then be used to hold device drivers and memory resident programs. This is covered in Chapters 5 and 9. The benefit? With device drivers and memory-resident software out of conventional memory, you have more conventional memory in which to run programs. Additionally, you can transfer the MS-DOS kernel (MS-DOS's own resident programs) from conventional memory into the HMA, leaving you with oodles of conventional memory for running your applications.

CONCLUSION

All this information—all the new terms and different types of memory—requires a special section to wrap things up. To recap:

- Conventional memory is memory from 0 KB through 640 KB. It's where MS-DOS runs programs. It's the only memory allocated in a PC for that purpose; MS-DOS cannot run programs elsewhere.

- For MS-DOS programs, expanded memory is the most important. Programs that want to access expanded memory can do so—but only for data-storage purposes. You cannot run programs in expanded memory.

- Extended memory is memory above 1 MB in an 80286-based or '386-based computer. MS-DOS can use extended memory for data storage, but you cannot run MS-DOS programs there. Programs written for Microsoft Windows can take full advantage of extended memory. In '386 enhanced mode, Windows can even use extended memory to simulate expanded memory.

- The memory benefits under MS-DOS are greater on 80286-based and '386-based computers. With those systems you can get an extra 64 KB of conventional memory by means of the high memory area (HMA).

- Using expanded memory and a third-party memory manager, you can fill in unused areas of upper memory with upper memory blocks (UMBs). MS-DOS can do this on a '386-based computer with extended memory. Into the UMBs you can load your device drivers and memory-resident software, freeing up that much-needed conventional memory.

SUMMARY

Memory in a PC is a confusing issue; a variety of terms are used to describe the types of computer memory and the locations for the computer's memory. There's no skirting around this: You must understand the terms in order to get the most from your computer's memory. Here are the most important concepts:

- All computers have RAM and ROM: RAM is used to temporarily store information; ROM contains permanent information that can be read by the microprocessor but cannot be changed.

- The original PC's 1-MB address space was divided into 640 KB for RAM and 384 KB for ROM and future expansion.

- Because 640 KB wasn't enough memory for some applications, Lotus, Intel, and Microsoft developed the LIM Expanded Memory Specification (EMS). This allowed EMS-compatible applications to access 8 MB of expanded memory, although that memory could be used only for storage, not for running programs.

- The EMS standard is the hardware and software specification for expanded memory.

- Memory above 1 MB on an 80286-based or '386-based computer is called extended memory. MS-DOS cannot run programs in extended memory. Extended memory can, however, be used by some special applications and for data storage.

- The XMS defines a software interface that enables 80286-based and '386-based computers to use extended memory.

- The high memory area (HMA) is the first 64-KB segment of extended memory on 80286-based and '386-based computers with extended memory. With the proper device driver installed, MS-DOS takes direct advantage of the HMA.

- Upper memory is divided into areas of ROM and video RAM, but most of it remains unused. On '386-based computers with extended memory, MS-DOS has the ability to map extended memory into those unused regions and create UMBs, which can then be used to store device drivers and memory-resident programs.

- The bottom line: Using the HMA and UMBs means more conventional memory for your MS-DOS applications.

Chapter 3

Peeking at Memory

Curiosity can be a passion or a passing fancy. Some people want to take apart a piano and see how it works, whereas others are content to play it. MS-DOS provides you with two commands and one tool to let you examine memory to the degree necessary to satisfy your curiosity. The two commands are Debug and Mem, and the tool is MSD, the Microsoft Diagnostics utility.

USING DEBUG

Debug is dynamite in a baby buggy; it's both powerful and simple. Using Debug, you can look at memory; manipulate memory; write small programs in memory; and load portions of disk into memory, change them, and save them back. We'll be using Debug to examine memory; it's beyond the scope of this book to get into writing programs or changing portions of memory.

1. At the command prompt, type the Debug command and press Enter. The Debug prompt—a hyphen—will appear:

   ```
   C:\>debug
   -
   ```

   (If you get the *Bad command or file name* error message, change to your MS-DOS directory and type the command again.)

2. To list the commands that are part of the Debug utility, type a question mark and press Enter. Figure 3-1 on the next page shows the result.

Looking at Memory with Debug's Dump Command

Debug's Dump command is the true memory voyeur: It displays the raw contents of memory on a byte-by-byte basis. To use the Dump command, type *d* and then press Enter. You will see 128 bytes of the PC's memory, arranged as shown in Figure 3-2. (Your values will be different.)

```
assemble        A [address]
compare         C range address
dump            D [range]
enter           E address [list]
fill            F range list
go              G [=address] [addresses]
hex             H value1 value2
input           I port
load            L [address] [drive] [firstsector] [number]
move            M range address
name            N [pathname] [arglist]
output          O port byte
proceed         P [=address] [number]
quit            Q
register        R [register]
search          S range list
trace           T [=address] [value]
unassemble      U [range]
write           W [address] [drive] [firstsector] [number]
allocate expanded memory        XA [#pages]
deallocate expanded memory      XD [handle]
map expanded memory pages       XM [Lpage] [Ppage] [handle]
display expanded memory status  XS
```

Figure 3-1. *Debug's Help command output.*

Memory address	Values of the 16 bytes at each memory address	ASCII equivalents of the 16 bytes

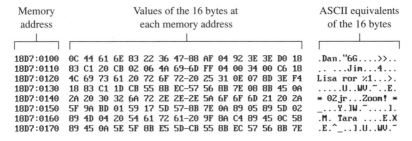

```
18D7:0100   0C 44 61 6E 83 22 36 47-88 AF 04 92 3E 3E D0 18   .Dan."6G....>>..
18D7:0110   83 C1 20 CB 02 06 4A 69-6D FF 04 00 34 00 C6 18   .. ...Jim...4...
18D7:0120   4C 69 73 61 20 72 6F 72-20 25 31 0E 07 8D 3E F4   Lisa ror %1...>.
18D7:0130   18 83 C1 1D CB 55 8B EC-57 56 8B 7E 08 8B 45 0A   .....U..WV.~..E.
18D7:0140   2A 20 30 32 6A 72 2E 2E-2E 5A 6F 6F 6D 21 20 2A   * 02jr...Zoom! *
18D7:0150   5F 9A BD 01 59 17 5D 57-8B 7E 0A 89 05 89 5D 02   _...Y.]W.~....].
18D7:0160   89 4D 04 20 54 61 72 61-20 9F 8A C4 89 45 0C 58   .M. Tara ....E.X
18D7:0170   89 45 0A 5E 5F 8B E5 5D-CB 55 8B EC 57 56 8B 7E   .E.^_..].U..WV.~
```

Figure 3-2. *The Dump command displays 128 bytes of memory.*

Each line of the Dump command's output displays 16 bytes—one paragraph—of memory. The display is broken into three columns:

■ The first column displays the address of the first byte.

■ The second column displays the 16 bytes of memory starting from the address shown in the first column.

■ The third column displays the ASCII characters that correspond to those 16 bytes.

Bytes that have no corresponding ASCII character are displayed as periods. The memory addresses and the byte values are displayed in hexadecimal.

Although the Debug information is intended for programmers, with patience you can discover the secrets that memory holds.

Type the following Dump command and press Enter:

```
-d 40:0
```

Debug will display 128 bytes of a low memory area officially known as the *BIOS data area.* Hidden among these bytes is the amount of memory in your computer, the number of disk drives in your computer, the keyboard buffer (an area where keystrokes are saved), the video mode, and the current time. Of course, this information is in hexadecimal and is not very obvious.

Now type the following command and press Enter:

```
-d fe00:0
```

Debug will display 128 bytes in the upper memory—in ROM. Specifically, this is the location of your computer's BIOS. You might see your computer's BIOS copyright notice as it's stored in ROM.

Getting a Handle on Hex

Debug uses hexadecimal (base-16) numbers. (Hexadecimal is often shortened to ''hex.'') Each hexadecimal digit represents a number from 0 through 15. Hexadecimal digits are identical to decimal digits from 0 through 9, and the letters A through F represent the numbers 10 through 15.

The numbers that Debug displays are all two-digit hexadecimal numbers, so they're relatively easy to translate to decimal— multiply the left digit by 16 and add the right digit. You will get a value from 0 through 255. For example, the hexadecimal number A3 is decimal 163 (10 × 16 + 3). The hexadecimal number FF is decimal 255 (15 × 16 + 15).

Changing Memory

As a memory tool, Debug lets you look at and access memory anywhere MS-DOS can look at and access memory. You can even change memory, although this isn't something you should do casually.

A good place for you to change memory is in video memory. Any changes you make there appear on the display for immediate feedback. Type the following Fill command and press Enter. (If you have a monochrome monitor, change *b800* to *b000*.)

```
-f b800:0 FA0 21 CE
```

This command tells Debug to fill FA0 (4000 decimal) bytes starting at location B800:0000 (B000:0000 on computers with monochrome monitors) with the byte pattern 21 CE. This command changes the background color to red and causes blinking yellow exclamation points to fill the screen. Why does this happen?

Address B800:0000 (B000:0000 on computers with monochrome monitors) is the start of video memory. An 80-column text screen (80 columns × 25 rows) has 2000 characters. However, it takes 2 bytes to store a screen character in memory. The first byte is the character's ASCII value—literally, the character to be displayed; the second byte is the character's screen *attribute*. (The attribute byte controls the character's color and intensity and whether the character should blink.) Therefore, an 80-column text screen is 4000 (FA0 hex) bytes long.

The ASCII character for hex 21 is an exclamation point. Screen attribute CE is a blinking character, with a yellow foreground on a red background. So this command fills the screen with blinking yellow exclamation points on a red background.

You can verify this by typing the following Dump command. (If you have a monochrome monitor, change *b800* to *b000*.)

```
-d b800:0
```

You will see 128 bytes containing the pattern 21 CE repeated over and over.

To return to a normal screen, exit Debug by typing *q* and pressing Enter. Clear the screen by typing *CLS* and pressing Enter.

Examining Expanded Memory

If you have expanded memory installed, Debug will let you work with it in the same way as you can work with conventional and upper memory. Most of the commands that access expanded memory (the *X* commands) deal with advanced memory concepts beyond the scope of our present investigation. However, the XS command lets you display the status of your expanded memory driver. Run Debug again, type the following command, and press Enter:

```
-xs
```

(You might need to press the Pause key to see the first part of the result. Press any key to continue.) Provided you have expanded memory in your computer, you will see a display similar to this:

```
Handle xxxx has xxxx page allocated

Physical page xx = Frame segment xxxx
Physical page xx = Frame segment xxxx
...
   xx of a total   xxx EMS pages have been allocated
   xx of a total   xxx EMS handles have been allocated
```

The xx's will be actual values. If you don't have any expanded memory, Debug responds with the message *EMS not installed.* This is all interesting and fun. But Debug doesn't tell you what you're looking at. It could be data stored in memory, a memory-resident program, a device driver, MS-DOS, or just some unused part of memory.

To quit Debug, type *q* and press Enter.

Note: If you are interested in exploring your computer's memory, check out The Peter Norton Programmer's Guide to the IBM PC & Compatibles *(Microsoft Press).*

USING MEM

Whereas Debug displays the contents of memory, the Mem command tells you what memory you have used; how much of it you have used; how much is available; what programs and device drivers are in memory; and how much total memory is in your system. The Mem command was introduced with MS-DOS 4—the first version of MS-DOS that actively supported both extended and expanded memory.

Typing the Mem command without any switches yields an organized summary of how memory is used in your computer. (See Figure 3-3.)

```
Memory Type        Total = Used  +  Free
-----------------  ------   ------    ------
Conventional        640K      44K      596K
Upper                91K      27K       64K
Adapter RAM/ROM     293K     293K        0K
Extended (XMS)*    3072K    1600K     1472K
-----------------  ------   ------    ------
Total memory       4096K    1964K     2132K

Total under 1 MB    731K      71K      660K

Total Expanded (EMS)            1408K (1441792 bytes)
Free Expanded (EMS)*            1024K (1048576 bytes)

* EMM386 is using XMS memory to simulate EMS memory as needed.
  Free EMS memory may change as free XMS memory changes.

Largest executable program size    595K  (609712 bytes)
Largest free upper memory block     64K   (65968 bytes)
MS-DOS is resident in the high memory area.
```

Figure 3-3. *The Mem command's output.*

There are five types of memory as you can see in Figure 3-3: Conventional, Upper, Adapter RAM/ROM, Extended (XMS), and Expanded (EMS). (You might not see all five types listed when you run the Mem command.) Notice that upper memory is divided into two parts. First Adapter RAM/ROM tells you how much of upper memory is used for various ROMs, controllers, the BIOS, and video RAM. The remainder (384 KB minus that value) is labeled ''Upper,'' which includes upper memory blocks (UMBs).

The Mem command's output also shows the total amount of memory available for each of the five types of memory. How much of that total is used (by programs, device drivers, RAM disks, etc.) is then listed, followed by how much of that type of memory is still available for use. At the bottom of the table you'll see a total describing how much memory is in your PC, how much you have used, and how much is available for use.

Note: *If 0 KB appears after Extended or Expanded memory, you don't have any of that type of memory in your PC. You'll need the right combination of hardware and software device drivers to have extended or expanded memory. See the sections titled "Expanded Memory" and "Extended Memory" in Chapter 2.*

Of all the numbers in the Mem command's output—and there are a lot of them—the most important is the value listed as the Largest Executable Program Size. This value tells you the size of the largest program MS-DOS can currently run.

Obviously, greed is the key here. The more memory you have available, the more you can do with it. But it's not simply a question of having 640 KB of conventional memory and 2 MB of extended memory. The issue is *how much of that memory you can use.* In Figure 3-3, the largest executable program size is 595 KB —quite a bit, thanks to MS-DOS's memory management prowess. That value can grow even larger, which is the point of this book.

The /Classify, /Debug, /Free, and /Module Switches

The Mem command has five optional switches. Four of them control the information displayed:

- The /classify switch provides a list of the names and sizes of all programs and device drivers in memory, and lists the largest available block of memory.

- The /debug switch provides an in-depth list of all programs, system data areas, installed device drivers and system device drivers (such as the printer and the clock) in memory and their locations and sizes (in both decimal and hexadecimal), and the total and available amounts of conventional, expanded, and extended memory in your computer. This is the unabridged memory display.

- The /free switch provides a quick summary of available conventional memory and any available memory in any UMBs.

- The /module switch describes the location and size of a specific program, device driver, or memory-resident program in memory.

The fifth switch is the handy /page switch, which is similar to the Dir command's /p switch. Because the output from the Mem command can be quite long, you can use the /page switch to automatically pause the display after each screenful of text. Type the following:

```
C:\>mem /debug /page
```

Press Enter, and you'll see the first screenful of information listing programs and installed device drivers in memory. (See Figure 3-4.) The four columns on the display tell you the memory location (segment) of every program or device driver in memory, its Total size in bytes (hexadecimal), the name of the program or device driver, and the memory type (what the memory is being used for—to store a program or a device driver, for example). Press the spacebar to display another screenful of information. The last screen is similar to the output of the Mem command when it is used without any switches, though a bit more detailed.

Only programmers and network administrators will need to use all the information produced by the output of the Mem /debug command, although you can type it to impress your friends.

The /free switch provides information about available blocks in conventional and upper memory:

```
C:\>mem /free

Free Conventional Memory:

  Segment           Size
  -------     ----------------
   0052B             80    (0K)
   01A9C         546432  (534K)

  Total Free: 546432  (534K)

Free Upper Memory:

  Region   Largest Free     Total Free      Total Size
  ------   --------------   --------------   --------------
       1    19120  (19K)     19328  (19K)     60480  (59K)
       2    13312  (13K)     13312  (13K)     65584  (64K)
```

```
Conventional Memory Detail:

  Segment              Total          Name      Type
  -------              -----          ----      ----
   00000              1039   (1K)               Interrupt Vector
   00040               271   (0K)               ROM Communication Area
   00050               527   (1K)               DOS Communication Area
   00070              2656   (3K)    IO          System Data
                                     CON         System Device Driver
                                     AUX         System Device Driver
                                     PRN         System Device Driver
                                     CLOCK$      System Device Driver
                                     A: - C:     System Device Driver
                                     COM1        System Device Driver
                                     LPT1        System Device Driver
                                     LPT2        System Device Driver
                                     LPT3        System Device Driver
                                     COM2        System Device Driver
                                     COM3        System Device Driver
                                     COM4        System Device Driver
   00116              5072   (5K)    MSDOS       System Data
   00253             10080  (10K)    IO          System Data
                      1136   (1K)    XMSXXXX0    Installed Device=HIMEM
Press any key to continue . . .
```

```
                     3104   (3K)    EMMQXXX0    Installed Device=EMM386
                     1488   (1K)                FILES=30
                      256   (0K)                FCBS=4
                      512   (1K)                BUFFERS=10
                      448   (0K)                LASTDRIVE=E
                     3008   (3K)                STACKS=9,356
   004C9               80   (0K)    MSDOS       System Program
   004CE               96   (0K)    COMMAND     Data
   004D4             2640   (3K)    COMMAND     Program
   00579               80   (0K)    MSDOS       -- Free --
   0057E             1040   (1K)    COMMAND     Environment
   005BF              176   (0K)    MEM         Program
   005CA             4672   (5K)    MSDOS       Free
   006EE             4144   (4K)    DOSKEY      Program
   007F1            88368  (86K)    MEM         Program
   01D84           534448 (522K)    MSDOS       -- Free --

Upper Memory Detail:

  Segment  Region      Total          Name      Type
  -------  ------      -----          ----      ----
   0C90A      1         816   (1K)    IO          System Data
                        784   (1K)    SETVERXX   Installed Device=SETVER
   0C96D      1          48   (0K)    MSDOS       -- Free --
Press any key to continue . . .
```

```
   0C970      1       27264  (27K)    SMARTDRV   Program
   0D018      1         160   (0K)    MSDOS       -- Free --
   0D022      1       17088  (17K)    MOUSE      Program
   0D44E      1      113440 (111K)    MSDOS       -- Free --

Memory Summary:

  Type of Memory          Total       =      Used      +      Free
  --------------          -----              ----             ----
  Conventional           655360  (640K)     32464   (32K)    622896  (608K)
  Upper                  158832  (155K)     45184   (44K)    113648  (111K)
  Adapter RAM/ROM        234384  (229K)    234384  (229K)         0    (0K)
  Extended (XMS)        3145728 (3072K)   1429504 (1396K)   1716224 (1676K)
                        -------             -------           -------
  Total memory          4194304 (4096K)   1741536 (1701K)   2452768 (2395K)

  Total under 1 MB       814192  (795K)     77648   (76K)    736544  (719K)

  Memory accessible using Int 15h         0    (0K)
  Largest executable program size    622800  (608K)
  Largest free upper memory block    113440  (111K)
  MS-DOS is resident in the high memory area.

  XMS version  3.00; driver version  3.09
```

Figure 3-4. *The output of Mem /debug.*

While the /free switch tells you what areas of memory are available, the /classify switch tells you which programs and device drivers are in memory and where they are located. This is the same information you can get from the /debug switch, but without the system device driver and other technical stuff to get in the way.

The output from the Mem /classify command can be quite long, so type the following and press Enter:

```
C:\>mem /classify /page
```

You will see a display something like the one shown in Figure 3-5, which tells you which programs and device drivers are in memory and how much space each occupies. The technical information you saw with the Mem /debug command isn't cluttering the display.

The output of the Mem /classify command is divided into two parts. The first part describes "modules" that are located in the first 1 MB of memory.

```
Modules using memory below 1 MB:

Name            Total     =   Conventional   +   Upper Memory
--------------  --------------  --------------   -----------------
MSDOS           57197   (56K)     57197   (56K)        0   (0K)
HIMEM            1152    (1K)      1152    (1K)        0   (0K)
SETVER            800    (1K)       800    (1K)        0   (0K)
COMMAND          3776    (4K)      3776    (4K)        0   (0K)
SMARTDRV        27264   (27K)     27264   (27K)        0   (0K)
MOUSE           17088   (17K)     17088   (17K)        0   (0K)
Free           589696  (576K)    589696  (576K)        0   (0K)

Memory Summary:

Type of Memory        Total     =     Used     +     Free
-----------------   --------------   --------------   --------------
Conventional         655360  (640K)    65664   (64K)   589696  (576K)
Upper                     0    (0K)        0    (0K)        0    (0K)
Adapter RAM/ROM      393216  (384K)   393216  (384K)        0    (0K)
Extended (XMS)      3145728 (3072K)  1114112 (1088K)  2031616 (1984K)
-----------------   --------------   --------------   --------------
Total memory        4194304 (4096K)  1572992 (1536K)  2621312 (2560K)
Press any key to continue . . .
```

```
Total under 1 MB    655360  (640K)     65664   (64K)   589696  (576K)

Largest executable program size        589296  (575K)
Largest free upper memory block             0    (0K)
MS-DOS is resident in the high memory area.
```

Figure 3-5. *The output of Mem /classify/page.*

(A module is a program or device driver.) The only way to tell whether a program is in conventional or upper memory (or both) is to see which of the columns furthest to the right contain its memory total. If both columns show a non-zero value, the module is located in both conventional and upper memory.

The second part of the Mem /classify command's output provides a detailed memory summary, providing both byte and kilobyte values, whereas when no switches are used with the Mem command, its output lists only kilobyte values.

The final switch is /module, which displays information on a specific program or device driver in memory. Here's an example:

```
C:\>mem /module doskey

DOSKEY is using the following memory:

  Segment  Region       Size      Type
  -------  ------   ----------------  --------
   010FA               4656K   (5K)  Program
                       ----------------
  Total Size:          4656K   (5K)
```

You must follow *module* with the name of a program or device driver. The /module switch tells you where the module is located in memory (a hexadecimal segment address that shouldn't concern you), its size in memory, and whether it's a program or device driver.

Don't sweat the /module switch. This is really a memory management troubleshooting switch. Instead, you should concentrate on the Mem command by itself and the /free and /classify switches.

The Root of the Problem

In Figure 3-5, you can see six programs and one Free memory area (an unused block of memory). The six programs are MSDOS, which occupies 56 KB; HIMEM, which occupies 1 KB; SETVER, which occupies 1 KB; COMMAND (really, COMMAND.COM), occupying 4 KB; SMARTDRV, occupying 27 KB; and the MOUSE device driver, using 17 KB. The Free memory area totals some 576 KB, all of which is available to MS-DOS.

The problem is that four programs—the MSDOS program, SMARTDRV, SETVER, and the MOUSE device driver—are occupying 101 KB of conventional memory. That memory is unavailable to any applications you run. However, a great untapped resource is waiting for you; the upper memory area has a potential to hold those programs, removing them from conventional memory and giving your programs more breathing room.

The solution is twofold. First you can move the MSDOS program out of conventional memory into the high memory area (HMA). Second you can move SMARTDRV and the MOUSE device driver, and any other device driver or memory-resident program, and "load them high," into UMBs and out of conventional memory. This is the essence of MS-DOS's memory magic (MS-DOS version 5 and above), and it's covered in detail throughout the rest of this book.

Other Mem Command Information

The Mem command tells you how much conventional, upper, expanded, and extended memory your computer has and how much of each is available. If you specify an optional switch, the Mem command also tells you what programs and device drivers are in memory, where each is located, and how much memory each occupies. The Mem command also reports on two additional items if they're available: the high memory area and any available UMBs.

Mem Command Tips

- All the Mem command's switches can be abbreviated by using only the first letter: /classify can be abbreviated as /c, /page can be abbreviated as /p, and so on.

- To obtain a hard copy of the Mem command's output, type the following command and press Enter:

  ```
  C:\>mem /c > prn
  ```

  Press the Form Feed button on your printer to eject the page. Substitute /d or /f for /c as needed.

The HMA is the first 64 KB of extended memory on 80286-based and '386-based computers with extended memory. When an extended memory manager, such as the HIMEM.SYS device driver that comes with MS-DOS, is installed, MS-DOS can access the HMA. Part of MS-DOS (the MSDOS program) can be transferred to the HMA, freeing precious conventional memory.

If you own an 80286-based or '386-based computer with extended memory and have installed an extended memory manager, the last line of any Mem command's output will be

```
The high memory area is available.
```

If MS-DOS has been transferred to the HMA, the Mem command reports

```
MS-DOS is resident in the high memory area.
```

If anything else is using the HMA, you'll see

```
The high memory area is in use.
```

And if MS-DOS is on a ROM chip in your computer, you'll see

```
MS-DOS is resident in ROM using the high memory area.
```

When device drivers and memory-resident programs have been "loaded high" into UMBs, you'll see them listed under the Upper Memory column in the Mem command's output. This is shown in Figure 3-6 on the next page.

Basically what's happened is that part of the MSDOS program has been moved into the HMA, and SETVER, SMARTDRV, and the MOUSE device driver (from Figure 3-5) have been moved from the Conventional memory column into the Upper Memory column. To do this, MS-DOS created UMBs, and then special commands were used to load SETVER and the MOUSE device driver high, into their own UMBs. (SMARTDRV automatically loads high if there are any UMBs available.) You'll learn how to do this in Chapter 6.

The total memory available to programs in the examples shown in Figure 3-6 now reflects memory available in both conventional and upper memory. The commands described in Chapters 5, 6, and 9 let you take advantage of this memory under MS-DOS.

```
Modules using memory below 1 MB:

  Name           Total        =   Conventional   +   Upper Memory
  -------------------------------------------------------------------
  MSDOS          15437  (15K)       15437  (15K)         0   (0K)
  HIMEM           1152   (1K)        1152   (1K)         0   (0K)
  EMM386          3120   (3K)        3120   (3K)         0   (0K)
  COMMAND         3776   (4K)        3776   (4K)         0   (0K)
  SETVER           832   (1K)           0   (0K)       832   (1K)
  SMARTDRV       27264  (27K)           0   (0K)     27264  (27K)
  MOUSE          17088  (17K)           0   (0K)     17088  (17K)
  Free          745360 (728K)      631712 (617K)    113648 (111K)

Memory Summary:

  Type of Memory        Total        =      Used       +      Free
  -------------------------------------------------------------------
  Conventional         655360 (640K)       23648  (23K)     631712 (617K)
  Upper                158832 (155K)       45184  (44K)     113648 (111K)
  Adapter RAM/ROM      234384 (229K)      234384 (229K)          0   (0K)
  Extended (XMS)      3145728 (3072K)    1429504 (1396K)   1716224 (1676K)

Press any key to continue . . .
```

```
  Total memory       4194304 (4096K)    1732720 (1692K)    2461584 (2404K)

  Total under 1 MB    814192  (795K)      68832   (67K)     745360  (728K)

  Largest executable program size         631616 (617K)
  Largest free upper memory block         113440 (111K)
  MS-DOS is resident in the high memory area.
```

Figure 3-6. *The output of Mem /classify/page after loading device drivers and memory-resident programs high.*

USING THE MICROSOFT DIAGNOSTICS UTILITY

Imagine a lovely pastoral scene. Maybe you hear the gurgle of water rushing by or the faint echo of a bird call. (Don't drift too far away.)

Using Debug to describe memory is like having a quantum physicist describe a pastoral scene in terms of quarks and subatomic forces. Using the Mem command to describe the scene is like having a chemist list the forest's compounds and their quantities. The Microsoft Diagnostics utility (MSD), on the other hand, would be akin to viewing a photograph of the scene. While Debug and Mem have their place, only MSD can truly tell you what's going on where in memory.

The Memory Map

The Microsoft Diagnostics utility is a handy tool that will tell you lots of detailed information about your computer. MSD is used primarily with tech support, to assist in determining your PC's microprocessor type, video system, disk drives, network, and other important information. MSD is especially descriptive about your PC's memory.

Start MSD by typing the following at the command prompt:

```
C:\>msd
```

Note: Follow MSD *with the* /b *switch to make the display easier to read on laptop computers.*

MSD will then display its main menu. You'll see a menu bar at the top of the screen and various "buttons" used to display panels of information on specific topics. Click the Memory button using your mouse, or press the M key. MSD's upper memory display will appear, similar to the one shown in Figure 3-7.

The memory display in Figure 3-7 illustrates a map of the upper memory area, the 384 kilobytes from the 640-KB mark on up to 1024 KB. The map is laid out in 16-KB banks of memory; each character in the map represents 1 KB of memory and each row represents one 16-KB bank of memory. You'll

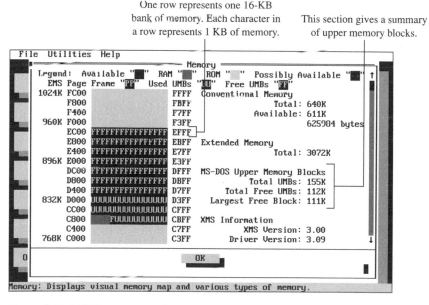

Figure 3-7. *MSD's summary of upper memory.*

also notice that the banks of memory are labeled using hexadecimal numbers. This might appear awkward, but memory utilities and the MS-DOS EMM386.EXE program (which simulates expanded memory while using extended memory and manages upper memory) also use the same hexadecimal numbers.

Press the PgDn key or use the mouse to scroll down the list until 640K (A000 hex) is visible. (If you're using the ANSI.SYS screen device driver and have the number of lines on your screen set to 43 or 50, you'll see the entire map at once.)

The bottom part of upper memory, from bank A000 hex through B400 hex, is probably marked with solid black characters, which means the bank is available. This is video RAM, where EGA and VGA graphics images are stored. The memory is available because it can be converted into usable RAM for programs. (You'll read how to do this in Chapter 9.) However, this chunk of memory is normally reserved for graphics images.

At bank B800 (bank B000 on computers with monochrome monitors), you'll probably see a polka dot pattern of gray dots on a black background. This bank is the start of *display memory*, the portion of video RAM you can "see" on the screen. (This memory was "filled" and "dumped" earlier in this chapter using Debug.)

Above video memory, usually at bank C000 hex, you'll see an area marked with solid gray characters. This is your video ROM and hard-disk ROM. Above that you might find solid black characters representing available memory, U's that represent used UMBs, F's representing available UMBs, or other interesting items labeled according to the legend at the top of the map.

The information on the right side of the map provides a summary you might have seen with some of the Mem command's variations. Pay special attention to the MS-DOS Upper Memory Blocks summary. This summary tells you the total size of all UMBs, the total kilobytes available in UMBs, and the size of the largest available UMB. This number can be important for figuring out memory management troubles in the future.

(If you don't have any UMBs, you won't see that information displayed; don't panic, you'll soon be creating UMBs.)

Memory Utilities

The upper memory display can be handy for getting a visual image of your PC's memory, and it can be invaluable for weeding out entanglements. But even better is MSD's Memory Block Display feature.

Using your mouse, choose Memory Block Display from the Utilities menu. (Or press Alt-U and then press Enter.) You'll see the Memory Block Display panel, as shown in Figure 3-8.

The right side of the panel is a memory map. In addition to the upper memory area, the memory map also displays conventional memory (locations 0000 hex through A000 hex). Each character in the map still represents 1 KB of memory, and each type and color of character represents the same type of memory as in the first memory map.

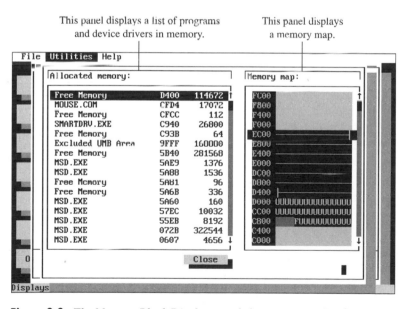

Figure 3-8. *The Memory Block Display panel shows you exactly where your programs are located in memory.*

The left side of the panel lists all the programs and device drivers in memory. This is the same information you'd find in the output of the Mem /debug command; everything in memory is listed. Even more interesting, when you select a program from the list on the left, MSD will highlight that program's exact memory location in the memory map on the right.

For example, if you have the MOUSE device driver loaded, highlight its name using the keyboard or click its name with the mouse. You'll see a bar on the memory map illustrate exactly where the MOUSE device driver is located, in either upper memory or conventional memory.

The two values following the program or device driver name indicate the memory segment where the program or device driver starts (in hex) and then the size of the program or device driver in bytes. (You can also obtain these two pieces of information using the Mem /module command, followed by the program or device driver's name.)

You can use MSD's Memory Block Display to help visualize where programs are located in your computer's memory, but that's about it. This tool is suitable for the curious and certainly better than trying to create a mental image of what's going on using Debug or the Mem command.

SUMMARY

Two MS-DOS commands, Debug and Mem, let you look at memory. Metaphorically speaking, the Mem command is for those who want to play the piano; Debug is for those who want to take the piano apart. The Microsoft Diagnostics utility, on the other hand, offers a detailed look at your PC's memory without taking it apart.

- Debug lets you examine or change memory, create small programs, load sections of disk into memory, save memory to disk, and perform other miscellaneous (and powerful) functions.

- Debug lets you look at bytes stored at memory addresses. (These bytes are listed in hexadecimal.)

- The Mem command tells you the total and available amounts of conventional, expanded, and extended memory in your computer.

■ The Mem command's optional /debug switch displays a summary of all programs and device drivers in memory and their locations, sizes, and types.

■ The Mem command's /free switch lists unused conventional memory as well as available UMBs.

■ The Mem command's /classify switch tells you—in an easy-to-read format—which programs are loaded into memory and how much memory they occupy. This information can be helpful in transferring device drivers and memory-resident programs into UMBs.

■ The Mem command's /module switch is used to report specific information on a particular program or device driver.

■ The Microsoft Diagnostics utility (MSD) can be used to graphically display upper memory, its ROM, RAM, UMBs, and other contents. The Memory Block Display panel will even pinpoint a program or device driver's exact location in memory to you on a memory map.

Chapter 4

Adding Memory to Your System

To take full advantage of your PC's memory potential, you might need to install additional memory chips in your computer. In this chapter, you'll learn all about memory chips: the obscure jargon that surrounds them, the shopping strategies that help you make a wise purchase, and the installation instructions that put them to good use.

ABOUT RAM CHIPS

Until you get to know them, it's perfectly okay to say that all RAM chips look alike. From a distance, they do. You could spend a slow weekend plugging them into the drywall in your guest bathroom for an incredibly interesting (albeit expensive) tile effect. Yet, upon closer examination, your visitors might notice that each chip has different markings on top.

Those markings on the top of a RAM chip are, in essence, your only clue to the chip's identity. As you saw in Chapter 1, a RAM chip is rated according to its *capacity* and *speed*:

- A RAM chip's capacity reflects how many bits it holds. (That's bits—not bytes.) Typical RAM chips store 64 Kb, 256 Kb, or 1 Mb. Because it takes nine of these chips to make up one bank, in the end you do wind up with a full 64 KB, 256 KB, or 1 MB of memory.

- A RAM chip's speed is measured in *nanoseconds* (ns), or one-billionth of a second—the time it takes a beam of light to travel about 1 foot. Slow RAM chips operate at 150 ns, medium-pokey RAM chips from 120 to 100 ns, and fast RAM chips at 80 ns and below.

When you buy RAM chips, you buy them in a bank of nine. Since most RAM chips are measured by the bit, that's eight chips for the 8 bits in a byte, plus one chip for a parity bit.

DIPs, SIMMs, and SIPs

RAM chips come in several different styles: DIPs, which are individual RAM chips; SIMMs, which contain one bank of RAM in a single handy package; and SIPs, which can be individual chips or multiple chips in a single package.

- DIP stands for *Dual In-line Package*. This is the most common type of chip: a flat rectangle, usually with 16 metal legs evenly divided between the right and left sides, as shown in Figure 4-1.

Figure 4-1. *A DIP RAM chip.*

DIPs plug into little sockets—much as Lego bricks fit together. But unlike a Lego brick, a DIP can be easily damaged—or even inserted in the wrong direction—while being plugged in. (Try explaining that to your 5-year-old.)

- SIMMs are a revolutionary concept for upgrading memory. SIMM stands for *Single In-line Memory Module*. Basically, a SIMM is a tiny expansion card, about half the size of a pocket comb, similar to Figure 4-2. Nine RAM chips—an entire bank of RAM—are soldered to the card. To install a SIMM, you simply plug in the entire SIMM card, gliding its edge connector into a SIMM socket (with the power off, of course).

Figure 4-2. *A SIMM RAM chip.*

■ Another style of RAM chip is the SIP. A SIP (*Single In-line Package*) looks like a mustache comb, as shown in Figure 4-3. Instead of having an edge connector (like a SIMM), a SIP has rows of tiny metal legs, which you plug into corresponding rows of tiny holes. Although a SIP—like a SIMM—contains a full bank of memory, its delicate legs make it much more susceptible to damage. Accordingly, SIPs are less popular than SIMMs.

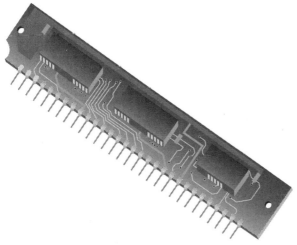

Figure 4-3. *A SIP RAM chip.*

Identifying a RAM Chip

All RAM chips, whether DIPs, SIMMs, or SIPs, have markings on top. These markings provide the following information about the RAM chip:

■ Its manufacturer. A company's logo or initials generally appear somewhere on the chip.

■ Its capacity. A number such as 1256 identifies a 256-Kb chip; 11000 or 1100 identifies a 1-Mb chip. Chances are that if a chip has the number 256 or 100, it's a 256-Kb or a 1-Mb chip.

■ Its speed. This value usually appears immediately after the capacity. A dash typically separates the two. Speed values are −15 for 150 ns, −12 for 120 ns, −10 for 100 ns, −80 for 80 ns, −70 for 70 ns, and so on.

■ Its proper socket orientation, noted by a notch or a dot on the chip. The notch should match a similar notch or dot on the chip's socket. If you install a DIP, you must pay close attention to the notch in order to properly orient the chip before plugging it in. (This is explained in "Installing DIPs," later in this chapter.)

Lots of mysterious (and unimportant) numbers can appear on a chip. For example, consider the chip depicted in Figure 4-4.

Figure 4-4. *A typical RAM chip.*

This chip comes from the Hollow Tree Manufacturing Company, noted by the distinctive logo. It's a 256-Kb chip rated at 100 ns. Notice the dot and the notch. That's the important information; the rest of the information is of use primarily to the manufacturer.

If you encounter a chip you cannot identify, seek an expert's opinion or take a guess. The number 1259 probably indicates a 256-Kb chip, with the 9 stuck in there for some unknown reason.

SHOPPING FOR MEMORY

About the best advice I can give for buying memory chips is the following:

1. **Know how much memory you need.** If you want to upgrade a PC from 256 KB to 640 KB of memory, you need 384 KB of chips—that's simple math. If you're adding expanded memory, find out how much memory your software needs. Also, you should be aware of the type of memory chips your PC needs. Your PC's motherboard might need one bank of 256-Kb chips and two banks of 64-Kb chips—or maybe even some unusual 128x4-bit chips. (Few computers require this type of chip.) Some expanded memory cards accept upgrades only in 512-KB increments (two banks of 256-Kb chips); some '386-based systems let you upgrade only 1, 2, or 4 MB at a time. Check your computer's manual or phone the computer company's technical support hotline.

2. **Figure out the number and capacity of the chips you need.** This again is simple math, but it also requires a knowledge of what you're upgrading. If the hardware requires DIPs and you need 512 KB, that's two banks of 256-Kb RAM chips, or eighteen chips. A 1-MB memory upgrade might require only one 1-MB SIMM. However, depending on your hardware requirements, your computer might need nine 1-MB DIP chips or thirty-six 256-Kb DIP chips instead.

   Note: Usually all memory banks must have chips of the same capacity. You can't add two banks of 1-Mb chips to two banks of 256-Kb chips and expect to have another 2 MB of RAM. See your computer's manual for details on the proper chip capacity.

3. **Know the speed of the chips.** The speed of the chips is totally hardware dependent; the faster your microprocessor, the faster (and more expensive) the chips you need.

   Note: The chip speed listed in your PC's manual is usually the optimum desired speed. If you plug in slower chips, you degrade the PC's performance slightly. You can even mix chips of different speeds within the same bank. The only drawback is that the memory bank operates at the speed of the slowest chip—possibly adding one or more wait states to the computer. My advice: Don't be cheap. Buy the faster chips.

The manual for your computer or expansion card describes the number, type, capacity, and speed of the chips you need to buy.

Understanding a Memory Ad

To be a shrewd shopper, you must be educated in the subtleties of reading memory ads. Consider the ad from Mondo Pete's Memory Emporium, as shown in Figure 4-5.

In Mondo Pete's ad, 1-Mb and 256-Kb DIPs are listed first, each according to its speed. A 256x1-80ns is a 256-Kb chip with an 80-nanosecond access time. Next come 1-MB SIMMs, also listed by speed. With SIMMs you need to be careful: Macintosh computers use SIMMs exactly like PCs do, but the Mac SIMMs contain only eight chips. Most ads use ''x8'' to identify Mac SIMMs and ''x9'' to identify PC SIMMs. Therefore, a 1MBx9-80 SIMM is an 80-nanosecond, 1-MB PC SIMM.

A memory upgrade kit is another option. Some memory merchants sell chips bundled as memory upgrade kits. If your computer is listed, you can buy the corresponding memory upgrade kit, which might be nothing more than four SIMMs rubber-banded together, plus photocopied instructions.

Normally all chip prices are listed. $CALL means ''The price on this chip changes frequently, so call for the current price.'' Remember that if you're buying DIPs, you need nine chips altogether, so multiply the price by nine.

Because memory merchants deal with memory full time, they're usually more open to questions than other over-the-phone hardware dealers. If your computer's manual recommends a certain type of chip that isn't listed in an ad, ask the dealer whether it's in stock.

One suggestion: Try to buy all chips of the same brand. This applies directly to DIPs. As you verify the capacity and speed on the chips, be sure they're all of the same brand. There's less chance of problems occurring if all the chips come from the same manufacturer.

Buy chips from places that will accept returns. Occasionally, a bad chip appears. It's nice to be able to get a replacement.

Figure 4-5. *A typical memory ad.*

And there's nothing wrong with shipping memory through the mail; most memory comes in static-free tubes. As long as your over-zealous letter carrier doesn't bend and stuff the tube into your mailbox, you'll be okay.

You can also purchase memory from the dealer who sold you your PC. If you're timid about adding the memory, he or she will probably even add the memory for you—but probably not for free.

PUTTING MEMORY IN A PC

The act of adding memory to your system is tinker-toy simple. You need only know which kind of chips your PC needs.

Note: The process of upgrading and fine-tuning MS-DOS for different types of computers is described in Chapter 10. The following information is simply general memory upgrading advice.

8088/8086 Systems

You can add only conventional or expanded memory to an 8088/8086-based PC: These microprocessors cannot use extended memory. If you already have 640 KB of conventional memory, your only option is to buy an expanded memory card. My advice is to buy a LIM EMS 4.0-compatible expanded memory card, regardless of how much conventional memory you already have. Fill the expanded memory card with as much memory as you can afford—at least 512 KB, but preferably 1 MB or more.

Next follow the instructions that came with the board to backfill as much conventional memory with expanded memory as possible, to create mappable conventional memory. You might need to disable some of your computer's conventional memory. This is done by changing switches on your computer's motherboard. (Consult your computer's manual for the location and the proper setting of these switches.) Configure any unused memory on the expansion card as expanded memory.

If expanded memory cards are out of your price range, your priority should be to pack your motherboard full of conventional memory. Some older systems could accept only 256 KB on the motherboard; the other 384 KB had to be supplied on memory expansion cards. See your PC dealer for such a card.

80286 Systems

An 80286-based PC can use conventional memory, extended memory, and expanded memory.

Most 80286-based PCs have sockets so that 1 to 8 MB (or more) of memory can be installed directly on the motherboard. The first 640 KB of this is conventional memory; the rest is extended memory. An 80286-based PC with 1 MB of memory on the motherboard has 640 KB of conventional memory and 384 KB of extended memory.

My advice is to use as little motherboard memory as possible. Disable all but 256 KB of your computer's conventional memory. Flip whatever switches tell the system that it has only 256 KB installed.

Next buy a LIM EMS 4.0-compatible expanded memory card. Pack that card full of RAM—at least 1 MB. Follow the instructions in the card's manual to configure half of the card's memory as expanded and the rest as extended. Then backfill the conventional memory that resides between 256 KB and 640 KB with expanded memory. (This creates mappable conventional memory that acts as one large page frame.)

Choosing an Expanded Memory Board

Chances are that an 8088/8086/80286 solution involves adding expanded memory to your system. That means you'll need to purchase a LIM EMS 4.0-compatible expanded memory card.

Many expanded memory cards are available. Two popular cards are AST's Rampage and Intel's AboveBoard. No matter which system you choose, be sure the card is LIM EMS 4.0 hardware compatible.

As for the special options available on some expanded memory cards (serial port, printer port, clock, game port, and so on), buy them only if you need them.

Adding memory to an expanded memory card is easy, primarily because you can (and should) add memory to the card when it's out of the computer. This is easier than adding memory to a motherboard (which makes you feel like a RAM-chip dentist). Note that some expanded memory cards require upgrades in specific increments of RAM (256 KB, 512 KB, 1 MB, and so on).

LIM EMS 4.0 allows up to 32 MB of expanded memory. Some expanded memory cards can hold only 2 MB, with room for another 6 MB on a special *piggyback card*, which costs extra. You'll need four of these expanded memory cards (with piggyback cards) in your system to get the full 32 MB.

'386 Systems

Users with '386-based systems have the best hardware for taking advantage of memory. Here the advice is easy: Buy as much memory as you can afford. Some '386-based systems will even run faster as you add more memory. My recommendation is 4 MB of memory, minimum. All of that memory will be used as extended memory in the system. Later you'll see how to emulate expanded memory with extended memory by using EMM386.EXE (MS-DOS's expanded memory emulator) or third-party memory-management software.

When adding memory to a '386-based system, be sure you use the special 32-bit memory upgrade slot. (The better systems will have these.) Avoid adding a memory expansion card designed for an 80286-based system; these cards "talk" to the microprocessor only 16 bits at a time, rather than the optimal 32 bits at a time.

Plugging in Chips

If you're going to add the memory, give yourself plenty of work space and good lighting. Get several sizes of Phillips and flathead screwdrivers and a needle nose pliers. Next turn off your computer, unplug it, and open the computer's case. (Refer to Chapter 1.) You will be inserting chips into either the computer's motherboard or a memory expansion card. If you're inserting chips into a memory expansion card, remember to do so *before* you insert the card into an expansion slot in the computer.

Note: Before you remove any cards from the computer or insert any chips, be sure you've discharged any static electricity you've built up. (Static electricity can fry a delicate memory chip.) Touch something metal, such as the computer's case or power supply, before touching any chips or cards. Try not to shuffle your feet on the carpet or pet a long-haired cat while you work at your computer. Also, do not touch the metal legs on a DIP or a SIP or the metal edge connector on a SIMM.

Installing DIPs

To install a DIP, follow these steps:

1. Slide one chip out of the tube.

2. Orient the chip so that the dot or notch is lined up with the notch on the first socket on the motherboard or memory expansion card. (See Figure 4-6.)

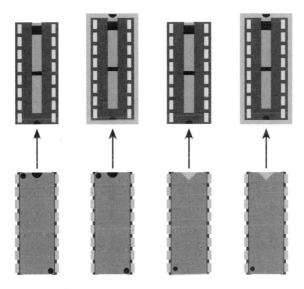

Figure 4-6. *Installing a DIP in its socket.*

3. Set the chip down on top of the socket.

4. Carefully check to be sure every leg on the chip is lined up with its corresponding hole in the socket. You might need to remove the chip and gently bend one or more of the legs to ensure a proper fit. (A needle nose pliers is handy for this.)

5. When you're absolutely certain each leg is lined up with the proper hole, press down firmly but gently on the chip until you feel it seat.

Note: Most chips are bowlegged. You might need to lay the chip down on its side, bending the legs slightly inward so that they line up with the holes in the socket. Use a flat, wooden object for this. (A Popsicle stick is perfect.) Avoid touching the legs with your fingers.

Always work on one bank of memory at a time in an orderly fashion. Take chips out of the tube one at a time. A wooden surface is best to work on because it doesn't conduct electricity.

When you've finished, inspect your work. Be sure that each chip is properly seated and that all the little legs are in the holes in the sockets. Sometimes one of the legs might bend out and away from its hole. You can remove the chip by alternately working a small flathead screwdriver gently under each end of the chip. Next straighten the leg with the needle nose pliers, and try to insert the chip again. (If this concerns you, buy a chip-insertion tool at an electronics store to make the job easier.) Note that the legs are fragile and can be bent only so many times before they break.

Installing SIMMs

SIMMs are much easier to install than DIPs. Follow these steps:

1. Slide one SIMM out of the tube.

2. Orient the SIMM so that the metal edge connector is above the slot. The SIMM usually faces chip-side away from the hook on each side of the slot.

3. Insert the SIMM at an angle into the slot on the motherboard or memory expansion card.

4. After the edge of the SIMM is in the slot, rotate the SIMM up until you hear it click into place. The hook on each side of the slot will pop into the hole on each side of the SIMM. (See Figure 4-7.)

There is only one proper way to insert a SIMM, so if it doesn't seem to fit, flip it around and try again.

If you're installing chips on an expansion card, plug the expansion card into an expansion slot in the computer when you've finished. After installing new memory, you'll probably need to set some switches on the memory card or on your motherboard to tell the computer about the new memory. Most PCs require that you manually inform them of the amount of memory in the PC. Check the manuals that came with your computer and the memory expansion card for the precise location and settings of the switches.

Figure 4-7. *Installing a SIMM in its slot.*

Leave your computer's cover off for now—you want to be sure the new memory works before you screw the cover screws back in. Connect the power cord, monitor, and keyboard—you'll need them to test the memory.

The Obligatory Error Message

If you've added extended memory to an 80286-based or '386-based system, you'll see a memory error message the next time the computer boots. This is because the computer "remembers" how much memory was installed before you added the new memory. Turn on your computer now, and ignore the memory error message. Run your computer's Setup program to tell the computer about the newly installed memory, and the computer will "remember" the new amount. You won't see the memory error message the next time the computer boots. Note that 8088/8086-based systems don't get the memory error message—these computers simply count up the memory.

You might see the dreaded *Parity error* message. This message usually means there's a bad chip installed somewhere. Tracking down the bad chip can be tough, unless it's improperly inserted or missing a leg in a socket.

Spend a few minutes looking for a bent leg. If you don't see one, you probably have a bad chip. Few diagnostic utilities can track down a bad chip because each PC has a different memory arrangement, so your best bet would be to call a technician for professional advice.

After you're satisfied that everything works, put the cover back on the computer, tighten the screws, and then reassemble your computer system.

Updating Your Software

The software side of the memory upgrade sometimes involves adding a new device driver. All LIM EMS 4.0-compatible memory expansion cards come with an expanded memory manager to control the expanded memory. Use the setup software provided with the card to install the expanded memory manager and configure the expanded memory.

Applications that can use the new memory probably will—automatically. Some applications might need to be informed of the new memory. If you're already using third-party memory managers, be sure to reinstall them or reconfigure them to work with the new memory.

If you're not using third-party memory-management software, device drivers and new commands give you access to this new memory. The next chapter describes installing the device drivers and using the new commands.

SUMMARY

Before you can take full advantage of your computer's potential, you must have plenty of memory. To add memory, you install RAM chips in your computer.

■ RAM chips are measured by their capacity and speed. The capacity is the number of bits the chip holds, typically 256 Kb or 1 Mb. The speed is measured in nanoseconds (ns): The lower the number, the faster the chip.

■ Your hardware dictates the type of RAM chip you purchase. A 1-MB RAM upgrade requires a certain type and number of chips at a certain capacity and speed.

- You can add memory to a computer on the motherboard (if there is available room), on a LIM EMS 4.0-compatible memory expansion card, or on a special memory card.

- A good upgrade strategy to use with 8088/8086-based and 80286-based systems is to buy a LIM EMS 4.0-compatible memory expansion card. Then backfill as much conventional memory as possible with memory on the expansion card, and configure any unused memory on the card as expanded memory.

- With '386-based systems, you should always upgrade memory by means of the motherboard or the special memory card that fits into a 32-bit memory slot. All such memory will be extended memory.

- Install chips with patience and care. Orient DIPs properly, and plug them in one at a time. (Be sure not to touch the legs—use a wooden object for this.)

- After installing new memory chips, tell your computer about the new memory; flip the necessary motherboard switches, and run the Setup program on 80286-based or '386-based systems. Then reinstall or reconfigure any third-party memory-management software.

Chapter 5

Optimizing Memory with MS-DOS

Having lots of memory in your PC and not being able to use it is like being 11 years old and ''grounded'' on a sunny day. This chapter describes how MS-DOS can help you get the most from your PC and your PC's memory. Special memory commands are covered here step by step. You can stop making improvements at any point or continue as your hardware allows.

Note: If you're working on an 8088/8086-based PC, the information in this chapter doesn't pertain to you. See Chapters 9 and 10 for comparable information regarding your system.

The Easy Way Out with MemMaker

MS-DOS 6 comes with an all-in-one setup tool that takes the manual labor out of memory management. The MemMaker tool is designed to configure your PC's memory and load your device drivers and memory resident programs into upper memory blocks (UMBs) to maximize the amount of conventional memory available. You simply type *memmaker* at the MS-DOS command prompt, and then follow the instructions on the screen.

The MemMaker tool is covered in detail in the next chapter, in the section titled ''MemMaker to the Rescue.'' You can turn there and use MemMaker to customize your system right now if you like. If you elect to do so, please turn back to this chapter and skim over the important information about what MemMaker does and how it benefits your system.

THE STARTUP DISK STRATEGY

In this chapter, you'll be implementing MS-DOS's memory-management commands—one at a time—by modifying your computer's CONFIG.SYS and AUTOEXEC.BAT files. You won't, however, modify the original files. Instead, you will copy the originals to a special startup disk. You'll boot with that disk to test new memory commands and configurations, keeping your computer's original CONFIG.SYS and AUTOEXEC.BAT files safe and sound on the hard disk should anything go wrong.

Creating the Startup Disk

To create the Startup Disk, follow these steps:

1. Create a system disk. Put a new, blank disk in drive A, and type the following command:

   ```
   format a: /s
   ```

   After the disk has been formatted and you see the message *System transferred*, remove the disk and label it "MS-DOS 6 Startup Disk." Place the disk back in drive A. Type a volume label for the disk and press enter.

2. Copy your CONFIG.SYS and AUTOEXEC.BAT files from your hard disk to the Startup Disk. With the Startup Disk in drive A, type the commands *COPY C:\CONFIG.SYS A:* and *COPY C:\AUTOEXEC.BAT A:*.

3. Use the MS-DOS Edit program to edit the CONFIG.SYS and AUTOEXEC.BAT files on the Startup Disk. Be sure all the commands and device-driver locations in both the CONFIG.SYS and AUTO-EXEC.BAT files use full paths, complete with the drive letter. (And be sure the search path listed in the Path command also uses drive letters and full paths.) Be sure to save the files when you've finished editing.

4. Press Ctrl-Alt-Del to be sure your PC boots properly from the Startup Disk. If it does, you're ready to start experimenting with MS-DOS's memory commands.

If you have problems booting from the Startup Disk, carefully examine any messages. There are two general types of error messages you might see: *Bad or missing XXXX* (where XXXX is the name of a device driver) and *Bad command or filename.*

The first error message means that you forgot to add the complete path of a device driver in the CONFIG.SYS file on the Startup Disk. For example, you might see *Bad or missing \DOS\ANSI.SYS*. In this case, you forgot to add the drive letter to the path for ANSI.SYS (C:\DOS\ANSI.SYS). Use the MS-DOS Edit program to make corrections, and then save CONFIG.SYS.

The second error message means that you forgot to add the complete path of a command in the AUTOEXEC.BAT file on the Startup Disk. If echo is on when AUTOEXEC.BAT executes, you'll see the command that causes the error message. To correct the problem, use the MS-DOS Edit program to insert the proper path in the AUTOEXEC.BAT file on the Startup Disk, save AUTOEXEC.BAT, and then reboot your computer.

Note: Echo is off if there's an @Echo Off command in AUTOEXEC.BAT. Echo is on by default.

If echo is off, you won't see the command that caused the error message. Use the MS-DOS Edit program to examine the AUTOEXEC.BAT file on the Startup Disk. If you can't figure out which command caused the error message, remove the @Echo Off command, save AUTOEXEC.BAT, and then reboot your computer. You'll get the same error message, but this time you'll see which command is causing the error message. Then use the MS-DOS Edit program to insert the proper path in the AUTOEXEC.BAT file on the Startup Disk and save the changes.

If the MS-DOS prompt doesn't appear for several minutes, remove the Startup Disk and reboot your PC from your hard disk. Use the Sys command to try to transfer the system files to the Startup Disk. (Put the Startup Disk in drive A and type *SYS A:*.) Verify that COMMAND.COM is on the Startup Disk. Then go back and edit the CONFIG.SYS or AUTOEXEC.BAT file on the Startup Disk to see what went wrong. If none of this works, return to step 1 with a new disk.

ACCESSING THE HMA

Most 80286-based and '386-based PCs come with 1 MB (or more) of memory. That's ordinarily configured as 640 KB of conventional memory and 384 KB of extended memory. Therefore, most 1-MB '386-based PCs can create the UMBs.

To seize control of extended memory, MS-DOS requires an extended memory manager. MS-DOS provides an extended memory manager device driver called HIMEM.SYS, which should be familiar to Windows users. (HIMEM.SYS was introduced with Windows 3.0.) HIMEM.SYS does the following:

- Makes extended memory available to programs that use extended memory according to the XMS (Extended Memory Specification)

- Prevents system errors that can result when programs make conflicting memory requests

- Lets 80286 and '386 microprocessors access the HMA

After HIMEM.SYS has been installed, XMS-compatible programs can use extended memory. Programs access extended memory using functions provided by the HIMEM.SYS device driver. Additionally, HIMEM.SYS gives MS-DOS access to the HMA.

Chances are that the MS-DOS Setup program has already installed the HIMEM.SYS device driver in your CONFIG.SYS file. If not, insert the following line on the first line of CONFIG.SYS on the Startup Disk:

```
device=c:\dos\himem.sys /v
```

Be sure to substitute the proper path if HIMEM.SYS is not in the C:\DOS subdirectory as shown. The /v switch tells HIMEM.SYS to display status and error messages when loading. You can remove this switch after you're sure HIMEM.SYS is loading correctly.

The only commands or device drivers that should come before HIMEM.SYS are special hard-disk device drivers, such as DMDRVR.BIN from OnTrak software or the ASPI4DOS or other SCSI hard-disk device drivers. If you are using a special hard-disk device driver, then position the *device=c:\dos\himem.sys* command on the second line of CONFIG.SYS.

Note: The command summary in Appendix B describes the options available with the HIMEM.SYS device driver.

The following is a sample CONFIG.SYS file with HIMEM.SYS added:

```
device=c:\dos\himem.sys /v
files=10
shell=c:\dos\command.com c:\dos\ /p
stacks=0,0
```

When you've finished installing the HIMEM.SYS device driver in your
CONFIG.SYS file, save CONFIG.SYS and return to MS-DOS. Reboot your
PC by pressing Ctrl-Alt-Del to test the Startup Disk. (Any time you
change CONFIG.SYS, you must reboot your computer for the changes to
take effect.) You'll see the HIMEM.SYS startup message after the computer boots:

```
HIMEM: DOS XMS Driver, Version 3.09 - 12/17/92
Extended Memory Specification (XMS) Version 3.0
Copyright 1988-1993 Microsoft Corp.

Installed A20 handler number 1.
64K High Memory Area is available.
```

The *A20 handler* is what gives MS-DOS access to the HMA. (If you're
curious, the HMA is accessed by enabling address line 20 on 80286 and
'386 microprocessors.) The message *64K High Memory Area is available*
means that MS-DOS now has access to the HMA.

If you see the *Bad or missing HIMEM.SYS* error message, you probably
specified an incorrect path for HIMEM.SYS in the CONFIG.SYS file. If
you see *Error in CONFIG.SYS line xx*, you probably made a typo on line xx
of CONFIG.SYS. (xx will be the line number.) Reedit the CONFIG.SYS file
on your Startup Disk, and reboot your computer again.

Which HIMEM.SYS Should You Use?

If you have Microsoft Windows 3.0 or above, you might notice some
duplication of filenames on your system. For example, both MS-DOS
and Windows have files called HIMEM.SYS, EMM386.EXE,
RAMDRIVE.SYS, and SMARTDRV.SYS. But which do you use?

Always use the newest device drivers. Use the Dir command to
check file dates, and use the file with the most recent date. The
reason? The newer device drivers often add more features and fix
bugs found in the older device drivers.

If you see any other messages, such as *An Extended Memory Manager is already installed* or *WARNING: The A20 Line was already enabled*, you probably have a third-party memory manager that's being installed before HIMEM.SYS. Remove the line in CONFIG.SYS that loads the other memory manager, or position the command that loads the other memory manager *after* the command that loads HIMEM.SYS in the CONFIG.SYS file on your Startup Disk. (Additional instructions for using third-party memory managers are provided in Chapter 9.)

Other messages might explain that your computer doesn't have an 80286 or '386 microprocessor or that your PC has no extended memory. In the case of the latter, refer to Chapter 4 for instructions on adding extended memory to your PC.

The major benefits of the HIMEM.SYS device driver aren't immediately apparent as far as memory usage is concerned. If you use the Mem command to view memory, you'll see only the following standard display. (The memory sizes shown below might differ from what's shown on your screen, depending on how much memory is installed in your computer.)

```
Memory Type        Total =  Used  +  Free
----------------   ------   ------   ------
Conventional        640K     90K     550K
Upper                 0K      0K       0K
Adapter RAM/ROM     384K     384K      0K
Extended (XMS)     3072K    1088K    1984K
----------------   ------   ------   ------
Total memory       4096K    1562K    2534K

Total under 1 MB    640K     90K     550K

Largest executable program size      550K   (563488 bytes)
Largest free upper memory block        0K      (0 bytes)
The high memory area is available.
```

This command tells you that there's a total of 640 KB of conventional memory and 3072 KB of extended memory, with 550 KB of memory available for applications. However, notice the last line, *The high memory area is available.* HIMEM.SYS has created the HMA, and now an extra 64-KB ''bank'' of memory is available for MS-DOS to use.

THE DOS COMMAND

The Dos command serves two purposes:

■ It moves part of MS-DOS from conventional memory into the HMA.

■ It prepares MS-DOS to create UMBs in upper memory on '386-based PCs with extended memory.

The format of the Dos command is

```
dos=high¦low[,umb¦,noumb]
dos=[high,¦low,] umb¦noumb
```

Options are shown in square brackets ([ ]). Mutually exclusive options (which means you can choose one or the other, but not both) are separated by the broken pipe character (¦). Multiple options must be separated with commas.

When you specify *dos=high*, part of MS-DOS loads into the HMA, which frees some 50 KB of conventional memory. When you specify *dos=low*, MS-DOS loads into conventional memory. The default is dos=low.

When you specify *dos=umb*, MS-DOS prepares to create UMBs that can be used for storing device drivers and memory-resident programs. If you specify *dos=noumb*, the UMBs are not created. The default is dos=noumb.

Note: The umb option works only on '386-based PCs with extended memory. The HIMEM.SYS device driver must be installed before this command can be used. If you have an 8088/8086-based or 80286-based PC, MS-DOS ignores the umb option.

To load part of MS-DOS into the HMA and thereby free some 50 KB of conventional memory, put the dos=high command into the CONFIG.SYS file on the Startup Disk. The dos=high command should go on the line following *device=C:\DOS\HIMEM.SYS*.

For example, the CONFIG.SYS file presented earlier in this chapter should look like this:

```
device=c:\dos\himem.sys
dos=high
files=10
shell=c:\dos\command.com c:\dos\  /p
stacks=0,0
```

Save CONFIG.SYS on the Startup Disk, and then reboot your PC to test the change.

After your PC boots, you'll see the HIMEM.SYS message. You might see the following error:

```
HMA not available : loading DOS low
```

This message means that another memory manager has loaded itself into the HMA, and MS-DOS was unable to load there. If this happens, edit the CONFIG.SYS file on the Startup Disk. Make HIMEM.SYS the first memory manager installed, followed by the dos=high command. Save CONFIG.SYS, and then reboot your computer again.

Here is where you hit pay dirt. Use the Mem command to see how much more conventional memory you have:

```
Memory Type         Total =  Used  +  Free
----------------    ------   ------    ------
Conventional         640K      42K     598K
Upper                  0K       0K       0K
Adapter RAM/ROM      384K     384K       0K
Extended (XMS)      3072K    1088K    1984K
----------------    ------   ------    ------
Total memory        4096K    1514K    2582K

Total under 1 MB     640K      42K     598K

Largest executable program size     598K  (612608 bytes)
Largest free upper memory block       0K      (0 bytes)
MS-DOS is resident in the high memory area.
```

The output of the command has changed slightly. Notice that more conventional memory is now available (from 550 KB to 598 KB). You're also told that MS-DOS is now in the HMA.

Preparing for UMBs

The second optional parameter of the Dos command is umb ¦ noumb. On a '386-based PC, when you specify *dos=umb*, MS-DOS prepares to create UMBs. By itself, dos=umb doesn't create UMBs, but it sets the stage for doing so at a later time. This will be covered later in this chapter.

On your Startup Disk, edit the CONFIG.SYS file. Look for the line containing the Dos command. Below it, add the following:

```
dos=umb
```

This tells MS-DOS to prepare to create UMBs.

Note: You can place both options on a single line if you like; for example, dos=high,umb. *However, by placing each command on a separate line, you allow for greater control with MS-DOS 6's interactive boot feature. (The interactive boot feature allows you to choose which commands in CONFIG.SYS are executed. This feature is activated by pressing the F8 key when your PC starts.)*

SIMULATING EXPANDED MEMORY

You'll soon discover that the greatest memory benefits exist for the '386-based PCs—which makes sense given the powerful memory-mapping capabilities of the '386 microprocessor. Only on '386-based PCs can extended memory simulate expanded memory under MS DOS. If you have an 80286-based PC, first skip to the section in this chapter titled ''Updating the Hard Disk,'' and then move ahead to Chapter 9.

There's one good reason to want expanded memory on a '386-based PC: A lot of MS-DOS applications use expanded memory. Spreadsheets, paint programs, word processors, and other applications can often use a few kilobytes of expanded memory.

There are two steps to simulating expanded memory on a '386-based PC under MS-DOS: The first is preparing for UMBs using the Dos command; the second is telling the EMM386.EXE expanded memory emulator to simulate expanded memory using extended memory.

Using EMM386.EXE

MS-DOS uses EMM386.EXE to simulate expanded memory by using extended memory on '386-based PCs. Despite its EXE filename extension, this file is a device driver and is installed in CONFIG.SYS.

The EMM386.EXE device driver has the following basic format:

```
device=c:\dos\emm386.exe [[memory [ram]]¦noems]
```

Note that many more options are available for EMM386.EXE. For now, only the basic options necessary for creating UMBs and using extended memory to simulate expanded memory are covered. For a complete list of EMM386.EXE options, see Appendix B.

The EMM386.EXE format lets you specify two basic options: *ram* and *noems*. If you specify both options, noems takes precedence. The noems option tells MS-DOS to create UMBs using extended memory without simulating any expanded memory. Use the noems option when you want UMBs and access to all your extended memory, for example when running Microsoft Windows.

The ram option creates UMBs and also simulates expanded memory. By default, EMM386.EXE simulates 256 KB of expanded memory. If you need more, specify the amount you need (in kilobytes) with the *memory* option. You can also make use of the memory option minus the ram option—this simulates expanded memory without creating UMBs.

The memory option is a number ranging from 16 (for 16 KB) through 32,768 (for 32 MB). You can simulate as much expanded memory as the amount of available extended memory in your computer. Remember, the HMA takes 64 KB of extended memory, creating UMBs takes some extended memory, you might have a RAM disk loaded into extended memory, and so on.

Adding EMM386.EXE to CONFIG.SYS

Edit the CONFIG.SYS file on the Startup Disk. To simulate expanded memory or to create UMBs, you must load the EMM386.EXE device driver *after* loading HIMEM.SYS. A good position would be immediately following the dos=umb command. Insert the following line:

```
device=c:\dos\emm386.exe /v
```

Be sure to specify the proper path; in this example, C:\DOS is assumed. Also, you should note that the name is EMM386.*EXE*—not EMM386.*SYS*. The /v switch tells EMM386.EXE to display status and error messages when loading. You can remove this switch after you're sure EMM386.EXE is loading correctly.

To properly configure EMM386.EXE, you need to think about your software and answer the following questions:

1. Do any of your applications need expanded memory? If the answer is no, such as when you're running Windows, skip to step 3. If the answer is yes, figure out how much expanded memory you need.

If you have a '386-based computer with 2 MB of memory, 512 KB is a good value. (If you're uncertain as to the amount you need, don't specify anything: As a default, EMM386.EXE uses free extended memory to simulate expanded memory as necessary.) Specify *512*, or the value you've settled on, after the EMM386.EXE command in the CONFIG.SYS file on the Startup Disk, like this:

```
device=c:\dos\emm386.exe 512 /v
```

2. Does your hardware or software require any specific EMM386.EXE options? If so, look up the options in Appendix B, and add them as required. You might also want to check your computer's hardware manual with regard to the page frame location.

3. Will you be using UMBs? If yes, add the ram option as the last item on the line. However, if you're using Windows or if you've decided not to simulate any expanded memory, specify the noems option. For example, to create UMBs on a '386-based PC and leave the maximum amount of extended memory for running Windows, add the following line to the CONFIG.SYS file on the Startup Disk:

```
device=c:\dos\emm386.exe noems /v
```

If you want to create the UMBs and simulate 512 KB of expanded memory, the line should look like this:

```
device=c:\dos\emm386.exe 512 ram /v
```

You can specify *device=c:\dos\emm386.exe ram /v* if you want to create the UMBs and simulate only 256 KB of expanded memory.

With the addition of the EMM386.EXE device driver, the sample CONFIG.SYS file would look something like this:

```
device=c:\dos\himem.sys
dos=high
dos=umb
device=c:\dos\emm386.exe 512 ram /v
files=10
shell=c:\dos\command.com c:\dos\ /p
stacks=0,0
```

Finish editing the CONFIG.SYS file, and save it on the Startup Disk. Reboot your computer.

After booting and after HIMEM.SYS's message appears, you'll see the display from the EMM386.EXE device driver on your screen.

```
MICROSOFT Expanded Memory Manager 386   Version 4.45
Copyright Microsoft Corporation 1986, 1993

EMM386 successfully installed.

    Available expanded memory . . . . . . . .   512 KB

    LIM/EMS version . . . . . . . . . . . . .   4.0
    Total expanded memory pages . . . . . . .   56
    Available expanded memory pages . . . . .   32
    Total handles . . . . . . . . . . . . . .   64
    Active handles  . . . . . . . . . . . . .    1
    Page frame segment  . . . . . . . . . . .  E000 H

    Total upper memory available  . . . . . .   91 KB
    Largest Upper Memory Block available  . .   91 KB
    Upper memory starting address . . . . . .  C800 H

EMM386 Active.
```

The display confirms the amount of expanded memory you have available (in this example, 512 KB). After that, a list of items describes the expanded memory manager device driver information. (This information is very technical; you don't really need to know what it means. But if you're curious, I recommend Peter G. Aitken's *The Essential Guide to MS-DOS 5 Programming*, from Microsoft Press.) Finally, information about the UMBs is displayed. In this example, 91 KB of memory is available for storage in UMBs.

If you've specified the noems option, the display from the EMM386.EXE device driver might look something like this:

```
MICROSOFT Expanded Memory Manager 386   Version 4.45
Copyright Microsoft Corporation 1986, 1993

EMM386 successfully installed.

Expanded memory services unavailable.

    Total upper memory available  . . . . . .   155 KB
    Largest Upper Memory Block available  . .   155 KB
    Upper memory starting address . . . . . .  C800 H

EMM386 Active.
```

Expanded memory services unavailable means that no extended memory is simulating expanded memory. However, approximately 155 KB of upper memory is available for storing device drivers and memory-resident software. (More upper memory is available when no extended memory is simulating expanded memory. This is because the EMS page frame is not required. Some PCs can gain access to extra upper memory even while simulating expanded memory; this is covered in Chapter 6.)

Simply creating the UMBs doesn't automatically increase available conventional memory; you must move a device driver or memory-resident program to a UMB before you notice the difference. However, the Mem command will alert you to the presence of the new memory:

```
Memory Type       Total  =  Used   +  Free
----------------  ------    ------    ------
Conventional       640K       18K      622K
Upper              155K        0K      155K
Adapter RAM/ROM    229K      229K        0K
Extended (XMS)    3072K     1396K     1676K
----------------  ------    ------    ------
Total memory      4096K     1643K     2453K

Total under 1 MB   795K       45K      750K

Largest executable program size        622K  (636960 bytes)
Largest free upper memory block        128K  (131504 bytes)
MS-DOS is resident in the high memory area.
```

The *Upper* memory line now shows something of substance: 155 KB of UMBs were created and all are available. Also, a greater amount of extended memory is used, both in creating the HMA as well as supplying memory for the UMBs. If you've created any expanded memory, you'll see its values in the Mem command's output as well.

Note: Don't let the Total under 1 MB *value fool you: There's still only 640 KB maximum for running programs. The value* 795K *in the Mem command's output reflects both conventional and upper memory. MS-DOS is not trying to pull a fast one on you.*

Including and Excluding Memory

Upper memory can be an interesting place. On most PCs, only small slivers of ROM, various BIOSs, and video RAM occupy parts of upper memory. The remaining regions are what EMM386.EXE fills with usable RAM when you specify its noems or ram options. Unfortunately, EMM386.EXE does a lot of assuming about what's ROM and what could be an empty region of upper memory. Oftentimes it's necessary to tell EMM386.EXE specific addresses where ROM is located. This is done by using EMM386.EXE's X, exclude, option.

For example, suppose you have a network adapter card installed in your PC. The card uses a part of upper memory to store its BIOS (ROM) and other information. According to its manual, the card uses a chunk of memory that starts at memory segment D800 hex and ends at segment DFFF hex.

Normally this hexadecimal memory-block segment information can be ignored. After all, it's all in hexadecimal and sounds so complicated. However, you must tell EMM386.EXE not to map any RAM into that area or you might lose control of your network card—or worse, your system might become unstable and crash. To tell EMM386.EXE about the network card or any extra ROM in upper memory, you use the X option:

```
device=c:\dos\emm386.exe x=d800-dfff noems /v
```

The EMM386.EXE device driver is now loaded with the noems option. The X option tells EMM386.EXE not to put any upper memory in memory segments D800 hex through DFFF hex.

If your system has more than one area of upper memory used by some type of add-in card, you need to use the X option to exclude those ranges of memory as well. The values must be specified in hexadecimal. Use the above format. EMM386.EXE allows you to specify as many X options as necessary, separated by one or more blank spaces.

Note: You can often obtain the addresses of various expansion cards in your system from their manuals or by phoning the manufacturer for technical support. The Microsoft Diagnostics utility (covered in Chapter 3) might also be able to locate ROM in high memory and display it for you in the memory map.

On the flip side of the coin is the I, include, option. EMM386.EXE can be a bit conservative when locating available upper memory. For example, it might assume that all of bank E is reserved for ROM, when that memory is available on your PC. To include bank E as upper memory, you would specify the I option as follows:

```
device=c:\dos\emm386.exe x=d800-dfff i=e000-efff noems /v
```

Be careful with this option! EMM386.EXE is very thorough about finding unused regions of upper memory. Only use the I option when you know without a doubt that a part of upper memory is not used by anything else. Use the Microsoft Diagnostics utility and double check your manuals before specifying a chunk of upper memory with the I option.

You can use as many I and X options as necessary with the EMM386.EXE command. The X options take priority.

Running EMM386.EXE from the Command Line

EMM386.EXE can also be run as a stand-alone program if it has been installed as a device driver. From the command line, EMM386.EXE provides either the current status of expanded memory support or the option to turn expanded memory support on or off. EMM386.EXE also enables or disables support for a Weitek math coprocessor (a special chip you can install in some computers that handles mathematical operations). The command-line format is

```
emm386 [on|off|auto] [w=on|w=off]
```

The first option is either *on, off,* or *auto.* On turns expanded memory support on, off turns expanded memory support off, and auto activates auto sense mode, in which expanded memory support is enabled only when a program requests expanded memory. The default is on. Note that EMM386.EXE must already be installed as a device driver; otherwise, this command has no effect. Also note that expanded memory support can't be disabled if UMBs have been created or if any applications are using expanded memory.

The second option is either *w=on* or *w=off* and is used to activate support for the Weitek math coprocessor. The default is w=off. As before,

EMM386.EXE must already be installed as a device driver for this command to have any effect.

Without any options, the Emm386 command displays the same information you see when your computer first boots—informative stuff, but not extremely practical.

Your computer now has the following:

- An extended memory manager (HIMEM.SYS)
- Access to the HMA for storing part of MS-DOS
- An expanded memory emulator (EMM386.EXE)
- UMBs

Of course, there's still potential. Part of MS-DOS is now in the HMA, but UMBs beckon. Putting device drivers and memory-resident programs in UMBs is covered in the next chapter.

UPDATING THE HARD DISK

Before you copy CONFIG.SYS from the Startup Disk back to your hard disk, make copies of the current CONFIG.SYS and AUTOEXEC.BAT files on your hard disk. Type the following commands:

```
copy c:\config.sys c:\config.old
copy c:\autoexec.bat c:\autoexec.old
```

That way, you'll have copies of these files if you ever have problems with your new CONFIG.SYS and AUTOEXEC.BAT files.

If you're satisfied with the Startup Disk's CONFIG.SYS file, put the Startup Disk in drive A, and copy the CONFIG.SYS file from the Startup Disk back to the root directory in drive C.

```
copy a:\config.sys c:\
```

Remove the Startup Disk from drive A, and reboot your computer. You're now one step closer to mastering memory on your computer.

SUMMARY

To optimize your computer's memory potential under MS-DOS, you start with HIMEM.SYS and the Dos command. If you have a '386-based computer, you also create UMBs and, optionally, simulate expanded memory by using extended memory.

■ MS-DOS's extended memory manager is a device driver called HIMEM.SYS. This device driver also gives MS-DOS access to the HMA on 80286-based and '386-based PCs with extended memory.

■ The Dos command loads part of MS-DOS into the HMA. This frees about 50 KB of conventional memory.

■ The Dos command also prepares MS-DOS to create UMBs on '386-based computers with extended memory.

■ The EMM386.EXE expanded memory emulator serves two purposes: It maps extended memory into upper memory, thereby creating UMBs; and it uses extended memory to simulate expanded memory on a '386-based computer.

■ If you need to simulate a specific amount of expanded memory, include that amount (in KB) in the line that installs the EMM386.EXE device driver. If you also want to activate UMBs, include the ram option as well.

■ If you want access to UMBs but don't want to simulate expanded memory, such as when you're running Windows, use the noems option when installing the EMM386.EXE device driver.

■ To prevent EMM386.EXE from colliding with your network adapter or other expansion cards or ROMs in upper memory, you can use the X, exclude, option. The X option directs EMM386.EXE to exclude a specific block of upper memory when creating UMBs. X is followed by two hexadecimal numbers separated by a hyphen, that specify the block's starting and ending memory segments.

■ The I, include, option directs EMM386.EXE to include a specific block of upper memory as a UMB. Normally this isn't required, because EMM386.EXE is very thorough about scanning upper memory. I is followed by two hexadecimal numbers, separated by a hyphen, that specify the block's starting and ending memory segments.

- After they've been created, UMBs can be used to store device drivers and memory-resident programs.

Chapter 6

Loading High

In the last chapter, you prepared your computer to work more efficiently by moving part of MS-DOS into the high memory area and by creating UMBs. In this chapter, you'll take full advantage of this extra memory by using two MS-DOS commands to free conventional memory: Devicehigh, which moves device drivers into UMBs; and Loadhigh, which moves memory-resident programs into UMBs. You'll also learn about the Mem-Maker tool, which can be used to automate the entire process.

Note: MS-DOS's custom memory-management tool, MemMaker, is covered in the section "MemMaker to the Rescue," toward the end of this chapter. Refer there if you're opting for the painless method of memory management. If you do so, please return here and skim over the other important information presented in this chapter.

WHY LOAD HIGH?

Consider the ultimate '386-based computer: a fast microprocessor, a fast hard disk, and an abundance of memory. You've carefully added several megabytes of extended memory, which can simulate expanded memory as needed using EMM386.EXE. Yet no matter how much memory you have, MS-DOS still uses only the 640 KB of conventional memory to run applications. It's that 640 KB of conventional memory that's crucial. Anything in conventional memory besides your application is a potential RAM waster.

To get more from that 640 KB of conventional memory, enterprising MS-DOS users have developed a number of tricks. Prior to the memory-management commands introduced with MS-DOS 5, these secrets included doing without some memory-resident programs and opting not to buy memory-hungry programs.

Managing that 640 KB of conventional memory without help is a chore. Part of MS-DOS can be moved to the HMA, giving you an additional 50 KB of conventional memory. But suppose you still want to install a network device driver and a mouse device driver and use a memory-resident pop-up calculator. And now that you have a little more memory, you think about using that keyboard-enhancer program that's gathering dust on the shelf. The basic problem still exists: You have to load those device drivers and programs into conventional memory, which cuts back on the 640 KB of conventional memory. Or do you?

Loading high is the process of moving device drivers and memory-resident programs out of conventional memory and into UMBs. This process lets you use those programs *and* keep most of the 640 KB of conventional memory for your memory-hungry applications—the best of both worlds.

Note: Because the Devicehigh and Loadhigh commands require the presence of UMBs, and because UMBs can be created only on '386-based PCs with extended memory, the techniques discussed in this chapter will not work on 8088/8086-based or 80286-based PCs. Refer to Chapter 9 for solutions specific to those machines.

Moving Programs

MS-DOS can transfer just about any device driver or memory-resident program into a UMB. To find out which potentially movable device drivers and memory-resident programs are loaded and how much free memory is in the UMBs, use the following command:

```
mem /c /p
```

Figure 6-1 illustrates the typical result.

In Figure 6-1 and on your screen, locate MSDOS, HIMEM, and EMM386 in the Conventional memory column of the listing. Although those programs are anchored in memory, any device driver or memory-resident program listed after them other than COMMAND is movable. In Figure 6-1, that includes the RAMDRIVE.SYS and ANSI.SYS device drivers and the MOUSE and DOSKEY memory-resident programs.

Memory-resident programs appear after COMMAND.
Device drivers appear before COMMAND.

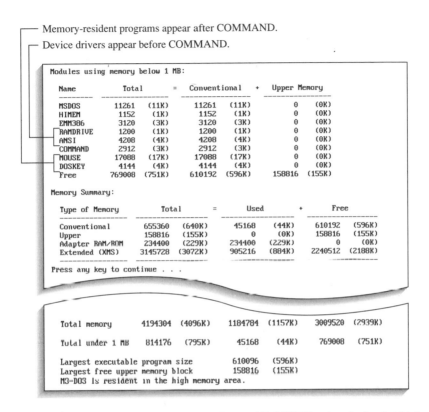

```
Modules using memory below 1 MB:

Name        Total    =    Conventional  +  Upper Memory
----        -----         ------------     ------------
MSDOS       11261  (11K)     11261  (11K)       0    (0K)
HIMEM        1152   (1K)      1152   (1K)       0    (0K)
EMM386       3120   (3K)      3120   (3K)       0    (0K)
RAMDRIVE     1200   (1K)      1200   (1K)       0    (0K)
ANSI         4208   (4K)      4208   (4K)       0    (0K)
COMMAND      2912   (3K)      2912   (3K)       0    (0K)
MOUSE       17088  (17K)     17088  (17K)       0    (0K)
DOSKEY       4144   (4K)      4144   (4K)       0    (0K)
Free       769008 (751K)    610192 (596K)  158816  (155K)

Memory Summary:

Type of Memory       Total    =     Used    +     Free
--------------       -----          ----         ----
Conventional         655360  (640K)    45168  (44K)   610192  (596K)
Upper                158816  (155K)        0   (0K)   158816  (155K)
Adapter RAM/ROM      234400  (229K)   234400 (229K)        0    (0K)
Extended (XMS)      3145728 (3072K)   905216 (884K)  2240512 (2188K)
--------------      -------          ------         -------
Press any key to continue . . .
```

```
Total memory       4194304  (4096K)   1184784  (1157K)   3009520  (2939K)

Total under 1 MB    814176   (795K)     45168    (44K)    769008   (751K)

Largest executable program size         610096   (596K)
Largest free upper memory block         158816   (155K)
MS-DOS is resident in the high memory area.
```

Figure 6-1. *RAMDRIVE, ANSI, MOUSE, and DOSKEY wait to be loaded high.*

By examining the information, you can determine if the device drivers and memory-resident programs will fit into a UMB: In the upper half of the display, you can see that RAMDRIVE.SYS occupies 1 KB; ANSI.SYS uses 4 KB; MOUSE uses 17 KB; and DOSKEY uses 4 KB. Near the bottom of the Mem command's output, you can see that the largest available UMB is 155 KB. Therefore, these device drivers and memory-resident programs can be "loaded high"—with room to spare.

All you need to do this are the commands necessary to load device drivers and memory-resident programs into UMBs. For device drivers, you need the Devicehigh command. For memory-resident programs, you need the Loadhigh command.

Note: *As in previous chapters, you'll be making changes to your Startup Disk before you actually change files on your hard disk.*

THE DEVICEHIGH COMMAND

The Devicehigh command loads device drivers into a UMB. Devicehigh works in the same way as the Device command. In fact, all you need to do is change most Device commands to Devicehigh commands—almost a search and replace. The syntax of the Devicehigh command is

```
Devicehigh=Driver
```

where *Driver* is the path and name of a device driver. This is where the Startup Disk comes in handy. Loading some device drivers into UMBs can be tricky, which is why changes made to CONFIG.SYS will be made first on the Startup Disk and then transferred back to your hard disk when you're sure everything works.

Your strategy will be to load one device driver at a time into a UMB, changing the appropriate Device command to Devicehigh. For practice, the first device driver to load into a UMB will be ANSI.SYS.

Loading ANSI.SYS into a UMB

1. Use the MS-DOS Edit program to edit the CONFIG.SYS file on the Startup Disk. Type the following Devicehigh command to load the ANSI.SYS device driver into a UMB (or edit the existing Device command for ANSI.SYS):

   ```
   devicehigh=c:\dos\ansi.sys
   ```

   Remember to specify the proper path for ANSI.SYS. (In this example, the C:\DOS subdirectory is assumed.)

   Notice how smooth the change was; you simply changed *device* to *devicehigh.*

2. Save the CONFIG.SYS file and exit to MS-DOS. Reboot the computer. The computer will boot as it did the last time you booted with the Startup Disk; ANSI.SYS offers no visual feedback when it loads.

3. Type the command *mem /c /p* and locate ANSI.SYS. This device driver now appears later in the list because it's loaded higher in memory. You'll see its 4 KB size specified in the Upper Memory column; 0 KB is specified in the Conventional memory column. This confirms that ANSI.SYS has been loaded into a UMB. You'll also notice that an additional 4 KB of conventional memory is now available in the memory totals.

There's one additional, easy test you can do to confirm that a device driver or memory-resident program has been loaded high. Type the following command:

```
mem /m ansi
```

That's the Mem command with the /module switch, followed by ANSI (the name of the module about which you'd like information). The output will look something like this:

```
ANSI is using the following memory:

  Segment  Region        Total       Type
  -------  ------    ---------------  --------
   0C93B      2         4192   (4K)   Installed Device=ANSI
                    ---------------
  Total Size:         4192   (4K)
```

The Segment column shows the memory segment into which ANSI.SYS has been loaded. A hexadecimal number indicates the memory segment, and any value that starts with a zero and is followed by a letter indicates that the device driver or memory-resident program has been loaded into a UMB. An easier way to confirm this is to look at the Region number listed in the output of the Mem command; only device drivers and memory-resident programs loaded high will be placed into a region of upper memory. For example, type the following command:

```
mem /m ramdrive
```

```
RAMDRIVE is using the following memory:

  Segment  Region        Total       Type
  -------  ------    ---------------  --------
   00253               1184   (1K)   Installed Device=RAMDRIVE
                    ---------------
  Total Size:         1184   (1K)
```

The output of the *mem /m ramdrive* command, on the previous page, shows that the RAMDRIVE.SYS device driver is in low memory. The Segment value starts with zero but is not followed by a letter, and no Region value is listed. Therefore, RAMDRIVE.SYS is still loaded into conventional memory.

Loading Device Drivers High

In the CONFIG.SYS file on your Startup Disk, locate another device driver, and change the Device command to Devicehigh. For example, to move the RAMDRIVE.SYS device driver into a UMB, edit

```
device=c:\dos\ramdrive.sys 512 /E
```

to read

```
devicehigh=c:\dos\ramdrive.sys 512 /E
```

Notice how the 512 and /E options (which create a 512-KB RAM drive in extended memory) are retained after the device driver's name. Start changing the Device commands in the CONFIG.SYS file on your Startup Disk to Devicehigh—but only one Device command at a time. Save each change to CONFIG.SYS, exit to MS-DOS, and reboot your computer to test the change.

After booting, check the results with the *mem /c /p* command. After moving the ANSI.SYS and RAMDRIVE.SYS device drivers, the Mem /c command produces the display shown in Figure 6-2.

Check out those numbers! 601 KB of free conventional memory is good— and getting better!

Continue experimenting on your own. But notice that in some instances, a device driver might not move into a UMB. Don't panic: The device driver loaded into conventional memory, either because there isn't enough room for it in a UMB or for compatibility reasons.

```
Modules using memory below 1 MB:

Name           Total       =   Conventional   +   Upper Memory
--------    --------------      -------------      -------------
MSDOS          11229  (11K)       11229  (11K)          0   (0K)
HIMEM           1152   (1K)        1152   (1K)          0   (0K)
EMM386          3120   (3K)        3120   (3K)          0   (0K)
COMMAND         2912   (3K)        2912   (3K)          0   (0K)
MOUSE          17088  (17K)       17088  (17K)          0   (0K)
DOSKEY          4144   (4K)        4144   (4K)          0   (0K)
RAMDRIVE        1200   (1K)           0   (0K)       1200   (1K)
ANSI            4256   (4K)           0   (0K)       4256   (4K)
Free          768992 (751K)      615600 (601K)     153392 (150K)

Memory Summary:

Type of Memory        Total       =     Used      +      Free
----------------    -------------      ------------      -------------
Conventional         655360  (640K)     39760  (39K)     615600  (601K)
Upper                158848 (155K)       5456   (5K)     153392 (150K)
Adapter RAM/ROM      234368 (229K)     234368 (229K)          0   (0K)
Extended (XMS)      3145728 (3072K)    905216 (884K)    2240512 (2188K)
----------------    --------------     ------------     --------------
Press any key to continue . . .
```

```
Total memory      4194304 (4096K)    1184800 (1157K)   3009504 (2939K)

Total under 1 MB   814208  (795K)      45216   (44K)    768992  (751K)

Largest executable program size        615504  (601K)
Largest free upper memory block        153392  (150K)
MS-DOS is resident in the high memory area.
```

Figure 6-2. *ANSI and RAMDRIVE are now in UMBs.*

UMB-Approved MS-DOS Device Drivers

MS-DOS comes with 11 device drivers. Most of these can be safely loaded into UMBs (but you probably don't want all of these device drivers loaded at once). The device drivers listed in the MEMMAKER.INF file in your MS-DOS directory should not be loaded into UMBs.

The RAMDrive device driver, RAMDRIVE.SYS, can be loaded into UMBs. However, any RAM disk you create won't be put into a UMB. For example, if you specify a 2-MB RAM disk—way too big for a UMB—only the RAMDRIVE.SYS device driver will be loaded into a UMB. The RAM disk itself will be put into conventional, extended, or expanded memory, depending on the RAMDrive options you specify.

Note: *MS-DOS's disk caching program, SMARTDrive, was a device driver in MS-DOS 5 and is now a memory-resident program. If you see a command that loads SMARTDRV.EXE in CONFIG.SYS, it's probably being specified with the /double_buffer switch. If so, do not attempt to load SMARTDRV.EXE high.*

Devicehigh Tips

- Use the Startup Disk to test loading device drivers into UMBs first. If your computer locks up, reboot from the hard disk.

- If you've modified the CONFIG.SYS file on your computer's hard disk so that loading a device driver into a UMB causes your computer to lock up, reboot and press the F8 key immediately after you see the message *Starting MS-DOS....* This directs MS-DOS to display a yes/no prompt after each command in CONFIG.SYS is read (but before the command is executed). Type *N* for the line containing the disrupting device driver. (This tells MS-DOS not to load that device driver.) After your computer boots, edit CONFIG.SYS so that line reads *device* instead of *devicehigh*, or refer to the device driver's manual for any suggestions.

- Change the order of the lines in CONFIG.SYS so that larger device drivers load first. Devicehigh is smart and will sandwich smaller device drivers into smaller UMBs when it can. But if you save your largest device drivers to be loaded last, they might not fit into UMBs.

- The optional /L switch can be used to load a device driver into a specific upper memory region. Use the *mem /free* command to locate an upper memory region large enough for your device driver, and then specify that region's number after the /L switch. (See Appendix B for the Devicehigh command's full format.)

- Use the MemMaker tool to automate the Devicehigh process. Refer to ''MemMaker to the Rescue,'' later in this chapter.

Keep On Going!

Continue modifying CONFIG.SYS to load your device drivers into UMBs, one at a time. Do this until you've totally optimized memory, loading as many device drivers as possible into UMBs.

After you're satisfied that as many device drivers as possible are loading into UMBs, copy the CONFIG.SYS file from the Startup Disk back to your hard disk: Put the Startup Disk in drive A, and type the following command:

```
copy a:\config.sys c:\
```

THE LOADHIGH COMMAND

The Loadhigh command loads memory-resident programs into UMBs. Although Loadhigh works in the same way as the Devicehigh command, Loadhigh is a bit easier to use. Here is the format:

```
loadhigh filename
```

filename is the path and name of a memory-resident program that you want to load into a UMB. (It must be a memory-resident program.) The filename is followed by any switches or parameters that would normally follow it on the command line.

Loadhigh is incredibly simple to use: You place *loadhigh* in front of any memory-resident program you want to load into a UMB, either at the command prompt or (more likely) in your AUTOEXEC.BAT file. To make life even easier, you can abbreviate Loadhigh as *LH*.

The strategy for loading memory-resident programs into UMBs is identical to the strategy for moving device drivers: Load the memory-resident programs one at a time, placing the Loadhigh command before the memory-resident program's name in AUTOEXEC.BAT. Then reboot your computer, and use the Mem /c command to confirm that the memory-resident program is in a UMB. Be sure the memory-resident program still works. For practice, the first two memory-resident programs to load into a UMB will be the Doskey keyboard-command line enhancement program and the MOUSE.COM program.

Loading Doskey and Mouse into a UMB

The Doskey program is a handy keyboard-command line enhancement program that comes with MS-DOS. In my opinion, every PC using MS-DOS should have it installed.

The following lines, which are part of your AUTOEXEC.BAT file, install Doskey and MOUSE.COM in conventional memory:

```
c:\dos\doskey
c:\dos\mouse
```

(Remember to substitute the correct path for Doskey and MOUSE.COM. In this example, the C:\DOS subdirectory is assumed.)

To load Doskey and MOUSE.COM into UMBs instead of conventional memory, add the Loadhigh command to the previous example in the AUTOEXEC.BAT file on the Startup Disk:

```
loadhigh c:\dos\doskey
loadhigh c:\dos\mouse
```

Save the AUTOEXEC.BAT file, exit to MS-DOS, and then reboot your computer.

After your computer boots, you'll see the message *DOSKey installed*, which tells you that MS-DOS has loaded Doskey. Confirm Doskey's location in memory by typing the *mem /c /p* command. Doskey should now be in a UMB.

In Figure 6-3, you can see that conventional memory is now completely devoid of device drivers and memory-resident programs; DOSKEY is now in a UMB, along with the RAMDRIVE.SYS and ANSI.SYS device drivers and the MOUSE.COM memory-resident program. All device drivers and memory-resident programs work, but they're located in UMBs rather than conventional memory. Comparing Figure 6-3 to Figure 6-1, the listing in Figure 6-3 shows 26,640 more bytes of free conventional memory, for a total of 636,832 bytes of conventional memory available to applications.

On your own computer, confirm that Doskey is in a UMB. If you're using any other memory-resident programs, such as third-party keyboard enhancers, print spoolers, RAM disks—even the venerable SideKick—

```
Modules using memory below 1 MB:

  Name          Total       =   Conventional   +   Upper Memory
  --------  ------------       ------------        ------------
  MSDOS       11229  (11K)       11229  (11K)          0   (0K)
  HIMEM        1152   (1K)        1152   (1K)          0   (0K)
  EMM386       3120   (3K)        3120   (3K)          0   (0K)
  COMMAND      2912   (3K)        2912   (3K)          0   (0K)
  RAMDRIVE     1200   (1K)           0   (0K)       1200   (1K)
  ANSI         4256   (4K)           0   (0K)       4256   (4K)
  MOUSE       17088  (17K)           0   (0K)      17088  (17K)
  DOSKEY       4144   (4K)           0   (0K)       4144   (4K)
  Free       768992 (751K)      636832 (622K)     132160 (129K)

Memory Summary:

  Type of Memory       Total      =     Used      +     Free
  -------------    ------------       ------------     ------------
  Conventional       655360 (640K)       18528  (18K)    636832 (622K)
  Upper              158848 (155K)       26688  (26K)    132160 (129K)
  Adapter RAM/ROM    234368 (229K)      234368 (229K)         0   (0K)
  Extended (XMS)    3145728 (3072K)     905216 (884K)   2240512 (2188K)
  -------------    ------------       ------------     ------------
Press any key to continue . . .
```

```
  Total memory       4194304 (4096K)    1184800 (1157K)   3009504 (2939K)

  Total under 1 MB    814208  (795K)      45216   (44K)    768992  (751K)

  Largest executable program size        636736  (622K)
  Largest free upper memory block        132032  (129K)
  MS-DOS is resident in the high memory area.
```

Figure 6-3. *DOSKEY and MOUSE are now in UMBs.*

experiment with loading them into UMBs as well. Remember to load memory-resident programs into UMBs one at a time, using the Startup Disk for testing.

Note: Although you can specify Doskey more than once in your AUTOEXEC.BAT file (for example, to create macros), you should use Loadhigh only with the initial Doskey command.

UMB-Approved MS-DOS Memory-Resident Programs

The first true memory-resident program was MS-DOS's own Print program, which first appeared with MS-DOS version 2.0. Since then, MS-DOS has played host to several memory-resident programs. Most of them can safely be used with the Loadhigh command. See the MEMMAKER.INF file in your MS-DOS directory for a list of programs that should not be loaded high.

The list of commercially available memory-resident programs seems end-less. Nearly all of them (those that can fit, at least) can be moved into a UMB, thereby freeing conventional memory. Keep in mind that Loadhigh isn't a miracle worker: If a memory-resident program is too big to fit into a UMB, Loadhigh will simply load the program into conventional memory. Do not use Loadhigh with non-memory-resident programs: The results will be unpredictable.

As with device drivers, the best way to find out which memory-resident programs will work properly when loaded into UMBs is to experiment. Use your Startup Disk until you're certain that every memory-resident program loaded into a UMB is working properly. Then copy the AUTOEXEC.BAT file from the Startup Disk to your hard disk. Put the Startup Disk in drive A, and type the following command:

```
copy a:\autoexec.bat c:\
```

Loadhigh Tips

- When Loadhigh can't load a memory-resident program into a UMB, it will instead load it into conventional memory. If this happens, experiment with changing the order in which you load memory-resident programs into UMBs before giving up trying to load that program into a UMB.

- If your system locks up intermittently after loading a memory-resident program into a UMB, disable loading the program by placing a REM command in front of the Loadhigh command that loads the program, and reboot your computer. If the PC stops locking up, edit AUTOEXEC.BAT to load the memory-resident program into conventional memory, save AUTOEXEC.BAT, and then reboot your computer.

- The MemMaker utility can be used to automate the Loadhigh process. Refer to ''MemMaker to the Rescue'' toward the end of this chapter for additional information.

MEMMAKER TO THE RESCUE

MS-DOS 6 comes with a memory-management tool for '386-based computers called MemMaker. MemMaker evaluates your system, then sets up the proper memory-management device drivers, and then loads your device drivers and memory-resident programs into upper memory. MemMaker does this automatically; you just sit and watch.

MemMaker might be the answer to your memory-management prayers, but it's not without its drawbacks. The primary advantage to MemMaker is that it removes the editing, saving, booting, and testing steps from MS-DOS memory management. MemMaker does it all. The disadvantage is that MemMaker keeps the memory-management process mysterious and cryptic. Your understanding of what's going on and how to fix potential problems is diminished.

Don't get me wrong: MemMaker is a great tool. Often it can configure and load high more device drivers and memory-resident programs than you could do manually by editing CONFIG.SYS and AUTOEXEC.BAT. Even so, I urge you to know the roles played by the HIMEM.SYS and EMM386.EXE device drivers, and the Dos, Devicehigh, and Loadhigh commands.

Note: If your CONFIG.SYS file contains a menu system (created with MS-DOS 6's multiple-configuration commands or with third party software), back up CONFIG.SYS before running MemMaker. Split your single CONFIG.SYS file into multiple CONFIG files (name the first CONFIG.1, the second CONFIG.2, and so on), each of which should contain a separate configuration. Place a REM command in front (on the same line) of the menu commands in each CONFIG file, so that only those configuration commands you want MemMaker to optimize will load. Then copy CONFIG.1 to CONFIG.SYS, reboot your computer, run MemMaker, and copy the modified CONFIG.SYS file to CONFIG.1. Repeat this procedure for the other CONFIG files. When MemMaker has modified every CONFIG file, reassemble the various CONFIG files back into a single CONFIG.SYS file and remove the REM commands in front of the menu commands.

If you don't follow this procedure, MemMaker might alter the configuration commands in more than one configuration section, or move commands that load device drivers to another section.

The MemMaker Command

The easiest way to set up MS-DOS 6 memory management on your PC is to remove any disk in drive A and type the following command:

`memmaker /batch`

Note: If you're using MS-DOS's DoubleDisk to double the size of drive C, you'll need to specify MemMaker's /swap switch, followed by the drive letter assigned to the original or "host" drive. For example, memmaker /batch /swap:d *would be specified if the original boot disk has been reassigned as drive D. This also applies if you're using the Stacker disk compression program.*

The optional /batch switch has nothing to do with MS-DOS batch files. Instead, this switch directs MemMaker to run unattended, without requiring any input.

MemMaker will evaluate your system, checking to see that the proper memory device drivers are installed and making a tally of CONFIG.SYS's device drivers and any memory-resident programs loaded by your AUTO-EXEC.BAT file.

Note: If a third-party device driver is in use, you'll need to disable it and reboot your PC before using MemMaker.

Information will flash on your screen quickly when MemMaker runs in the batch mode. By itself, your PC will be rebooted two or three times as MemMaker tests various upper memory configurations and tries to load as many device drivers and memory-resident programs into UMBs as it can. After the testing is completed, you'll be returned to the command prompt. Use the Mem command to see how much additional conventional memory has been made available.

Step-by-Step MemMaker

MemMaker is quick and painless when run in the batch mode; however, you miss a lot of the feedback it has to offer—including the end summary that details how much additional memory has been made available. Without the /batch switch, the MemMaker command displays that information, presents various options, and allows you to select the way you want memory configured. You might still need to specify the /swap or other switches, depending on your PC's configuration; refer to Appendix B for a full list of MemMaker's options.

To progress through MemMaker's various displays as it is running, press the Enter key. Press the Spacebar to change a selection. Pressing the F3 key quits MemMaker.

One of the first screens you'll see asks if you want the Custom or the Express memory setup. The Express setup is the one selected when Mem-Maker runs in the batch mode, and will most likely be the option best suited to the majority of MS-DOS users. The Custom setup is for experienced users; it allows you to set various advanced options, as shown in Figure 6-4.

If you're an experienced user and choose the Custom setup, I recommend setting only those advanced options you're familiar with. For example, if you know the monochrome region of upper memory (segments B000 hex through B7FF hex) isn't used by any of your programs, you can direct MemMaker to let MS-DOS use that region for running programs. However, this isn't recommended if you're running Windows. (The upper

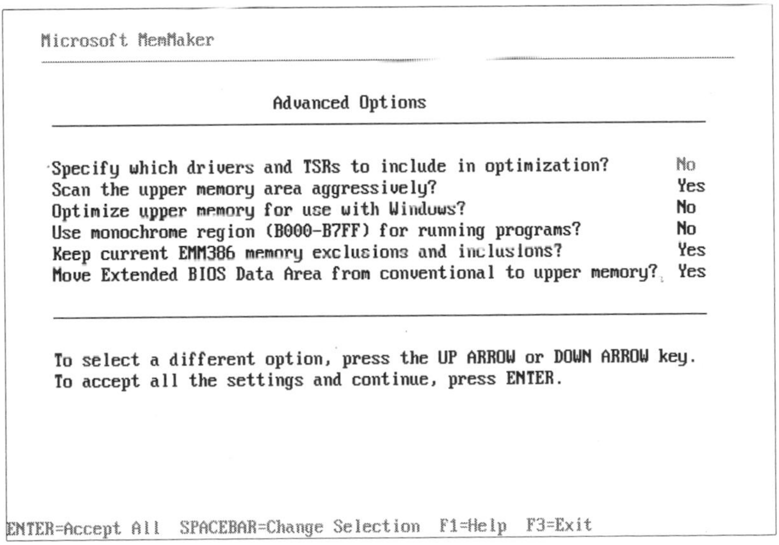

```
 Microsoft MemMaker


                        Advanced Options
 ─────────────────────────────────────────────────────────────

 Specify which drivers and TSRs to include in optimization?      No
 Scan the upper memory area aggressively?                        Yes
 Optimize upper memory for use with Windows?                     No
 Use monochrome region (B000-B7FF) for running programs?         No
 Keep current EMM386 memory exclusions and inclusions?           Yes
 Move Extended BIOS Data Area from conventional to upper memory? Yes

 ─────────────────────────────────────────────────────────────


      To select a different option, press the UP ARROW or DOWN ARROW key.
      To accept all the settings and continue, press ENTER.




 ENTER=Accept All  SPACEBAR=Change Selection  F1=Help  F3=Exit
```

Figure 6-4. *MemMaker's advanced options menu.*

memory is created with extended memory; Windows needs as much extended memory as possible.) If you're uncertain about setting any of these options, don't mess with them! Table 6-1 describes what each option does and offers suggestions on the setting.

Option	Description/suggestion
Specify which device drivers and TSRs to include during optimization	MemMaker will ask yes or no, pausing after each device driver or potential memory-resident program in both CONFIG.SYS and AUTOEXEC.BAT. Only select Yes if you know what is and isn't a memory-resident program and want to choose which device drivers and memory-resident programs are to be loaded into UMBs.
Scan upper memory aggressively	Selecting Yes here might yield more usable upper memory. On some PCs, however, this option might cause your system to crash. If your computer crashes after running MemMaker with this option set to Yes, run MemMaker again and set this option to No.
Optimize upper memory for Windows	Select Yes if you use Microsoft Windows.
Use monochrome memory region for running programs	Do not select Yes if you use Microsoft Windows.
Keep EMM386 excludes and includes	Only select Yes if you use EMM386.EXE's X or I options to exclude or include portions of upper memory.
Move extended BIOS area to upper memory	Only select No if you've tried this option and your system crashed.

Table 6-1. *Suggested settings for MemMaker's advanced options.*

After MemMaker has taken a serious look at your PC's configuration, and has checked for the presence of Microsoft Windows, you'll be alerted that your system will reboot. Remove any floppy disks from drive A, and then press Enter to reboot your PC and continue the MemMaker process.

After your PC reboots, MemMaker will evaluate the different ways your device drivers and memory-resident programs can be loaded into upper memory. MemMaker will figure out the best fit, and then reboot your computer again. You will be asked if your system is working properly. If there are no problems, select Yes and continue. Otherwise, you'll be alerted to the problem and given the opportunity to cancel MemMaker and undo its changes. (I would suggest rerunning MemMaker and selecting the Specify Which Drivers And TSRs To Include In Optimization item from the advanced options menu. Then skip over the problem program during optimization.)

When MemMaker has finished its job, it will display a summary of conventional and upper memory totals. You'll see a remarkable improvement in the conventional memory totals. Press Enter to exit MemMaker.

After MemMaker has optimized your system, there should be no need to further wrangle with your device drivers or memory-resident programs. You'll notice that MemMaker has inserted the appropriate Devicehigh or Loadhigh command in CONFIG.SYS or AUTOEXEC.BAT, usually with the /L switch to customize upper memory loading (described in Appendix B). Don't alter any of those commands!

When you add a device driver or new memory-resident program to your CONFIG.SYS or AUTOEXEC.BAT files in the future, simply run MemMaker again. It will reevaluate your system and add the device driver or memory-resident program to upper memory as best it can.

Note: MemMaker backs up your original CONFIG.SYS and AUTOEXEC.BAT files to your MS-DOS subdirectory and gives each the UMB extension. These files can be restored by running MemMaker with its /undo switch, or you can manually copy them back to drive C's root directory (with the names CONFIG.SYS and AUTOEXEC.BAT) and reboot your PC.

SUMMARY

You can take advantage of UMBs to load device drivers and memory-resident programs into the upper memory area, leaving more conventional memory for your memory-hungry applications.

- UMBs are created on '386-based computers by three commands in your CONFIG.SYS file:

```
device=c:\dos\himem.sys
dos=umb
device=c:\dos\emm386.exe noems
```

■ The command that loads the EMM386.EXE device driver must have either the ram or noems option after it to create the UMBs. If you specify the ram option, EMM386.EXE uses extended memory to simulate expanded memory in addition to creating the UMBs. If the noems option is specified, the UMBs are created, but EMM386.EXE does not simulate any expanded memory. (noems is the option to use for running Windows.)

■ After you've created UMBs, you can use the Devicehigh and Loadhigh commands to load device drivers and memory-resident programs into the UMBs.

■ The Devicehigh command loads device drivers into UMBs. Devicehigh is used exactly like the Device command in a CONFIG.SYS file.

■ A good strategy to take with loading device drivers into UMBs is to load the larger ones first.

■ The Loadhigh command loads memory-resident programs into UMBs. You simply place Loadhigh, or LH, in front of the command that loads the memory-resident program, either in AUTOEXEC.BAT or on the command line.

■ MS-DOS 6's MemMaker tool offers a one-step method of optimizing memory and loading device drivers and memory-resident programs high. MemMaker examines your system, sets up HIMEM.SYS and EMM386.EXE, and then proceeds to use the Dos, Devicehigh, and Loadhigh commands to load as many device drivers and memory-resident programs into upper memory as it can.

Chapter 7

Using a RAM Disk and a Disk Cache

Don't get caught thinking "I bought too much memory. I have nothing to do with it." Rest assured: There's always something you can do with extra memory. Even if your applications use only a small portion of memory, you can put the remainder to good use by creating a RAM disk or a disk cache to enhance the speed of disk operations.

WHAT IS A RAM DISK?

A RAM disk is an area of memory that behaves like a very fast disk drive. You don't need special hardware to install a RAM disk. You need only a device driver that convinces MS-DOS to treat a portion of memory as if it were a disk drive.

You can use a RAM disk as you would any other type of disk drive: You can copy files to and from it, give others access to it over a network, make subdirectories on it, and so on. You can't, however, format a RAM disk.

The biggest advantage of using a RAM disk is speed. Because a RAM disk is an area of memory, it is many times faster than a real disk drive—even faster than a hard disk. And because it has no moving parts, a RAM disk can save wear and tear on your real disk drives.

A RAM disk has two disadvantages. The first disadvantage is that it uses some of your computer's memory. A 512-KB RAM disk uses 512 KB of memory (although this memory can be conventional, expanded, or extended memory).

The second disadvantage is that a RAM disk is volatile. If you turn off or reboot the computer, or if the power goes off, information on the RAM disk is lost. This might not seem to be a big disadvantage—until you've lost a file that you've worked on for hours.

If you have extra memory and are careful about backing up important data on a floppy disk or a hard disk, the advantages of a RAM disk far outweigh the disadvantages.

INSTALLING THE RAMDRIVE.SYS DEVICE DRIVER

The MS-DOS device driver that creates a RAM disk is RAMDRIVE.SYS. You can create as many RAM disks as your computer's memory can handle. Simply load the RAMDRIVE.SYS device driver once for each RAM disk you want to create. The RAMDRIVE.SYS device driver is loaded with the Device command in your CONFIG.SYS file. The format is

```
device=c:\dos\ramdrive.sys [size[sector[entries]]] [/e:/a]
```

You must specify the correct path to RAMDRIVE.SYS. In this example, RAMDRIVE.SYS is assumed to be in your C:\DOS subdirectory.

size is the size of the RAM disk in kilobytes. Values for *size* range from 4 through 32,767 for a 4-KB through 32-MB RAM disk. (The size of the RAM disk is limited by the amount of memory in your computer.) When *size* isn't specified, a 64-KB RAM disk is created.

sector is the size of the RAM disk's sectors in bytes. (A sector is a unit of disk storage. A small sector size is good for storing small files, and a large sector size is good for storing large files.) Values for *sector* can be 128, 256, or the default of 512. (512 is the standard size of sectors on floppies and hard disks.) You must specify a *size* value if you specify a *sector* value.

entries indicates the number of directory entries RAMDRIVE.SYS will create in the RAM disk's root directory. (A directory entry is a place where MS-DOS stores filenames. If you specify 64 for *entries*, MS-DOS can store 64 files in the root directory of the RAM disk.) Values for *entries* range from 2 through 1024, with a default of 64. You must specify *size* and *sector* values if you specify an *entries* value.

The /e or /a switches (use one or the other—not both) direct RAMDRIVE.SYS to create the RAM disk in extended or expanded memory. If these switches are omitted, the RAM disk is created in conventional memory.

You can create as many RAM disks as your computer's memory will support. The letter MS-DOS assigns to a RAM disk will always be one letter higher than the last drive in your computer (up through Z). (Each drive letter uses about 80 bytes of conventional memory.) If you have drives A, B, and C, the RAM disk will be drive D. If you have drives through the letter H, the RAM disk will be drive I.

Note: *The Lastdrive configuration command is not required to set aside high drive letters for RAM drives. Lastdrive is only necessary for network drives, DoubleDisk drives, and drives created by the Subst command.*

Creating a RAM Disk

Creating a RAM disk is painless. For the memory it uses, the benefits to your computer can be great—especially if you have enough memory for a RAM disk over 1 MB in size. For practice, create a 64-KB RAM disk in conventional, extended, or expanded memory—whichever type of memory your computer has.

First decide what type of memory the RAM disk will use. Use the Mem command to find out the amount of extended, expanded, and conventional memory available on your computer. For example, on my computer, I see the following:

```
Memory Type      Total =  Used  +  Free
----------------  ------   ------   ------
Conventional      640K      18K      622K
Upper             155K      27K      128K
Adapter RAM/ROM   229K     229K        0K
Extended (XMS)   3072K    1396K     1676K
----------------  ------   ------   ------
Total memory     4096K    1670K     2426K

Total under 1 MB  795K      45K      750K

Largest executable program size       622K  (636736 bytes)
Largest free upper memory block       128K  (131504 bytes)
MS-DOS is resident in the high memory area.
```

My computer has 1676 KB of extended memory but no expanded memory. A 64-KB RAM disk can be created in conventional or extended memory on my computer, but I'll create a RAM disk in extended memory because I don't run any applications that use extended memory. Make a similar decision for your own computer. If you don't have enough extended or expanded memory, simply use conventional memory for this test. (64 KB is not much lost memory.)

Use the MS-DOS Edit program to insert the following line at the bottom of your CONFIG.SYS file:

```
device=c:\dos\ramdrive.sys /e
```

Specify the correct path for RAMDRIVE.SYS; unless you've moved RAMDRIVE.SYS, it's in your MS-DOS subdirectory, which should be specified after *device=*. In this example, the C:\DOS subdirectory is assumed.

The above command creates a 64-KB RAM disk in extended memory. If you have expanded memory to spare, add the /a switch, instead of the /e switch, to the end of the command; if you'd rather create the RAM disk in conventional memory, leave off the /e and /a switches. On my system, I've used the /e switch to create the 64-KB RAM disk in extended memory.

Save your CONFIG.SYS file, exit to MS-DOS, and then reboot your computer.

As your computer boots, you'll see the RAMDRIVE.SYS startup message:

```
Microsoft RAMDrive version 3.07 virtual disk D:
    Disk size: 64k
    Sector size: 512 bytes
    Allocation unit: 1 sectors
    Directory entries: 64
```

Above, the RAM disk is drive D. (Your RAM disk might be a different letter; watch the RAMDRIVE.SYS startup message to find out which drive letter MS-DOS assigns to your RAM disk.) Although the RAM disk doesn't contain any files yet, it does have the volume label MS-RAMDRIVE.

Confirm the RAM disk's size with the Chkdsk command. Type

```
chkdsk d:
```

(This command assumes your RAM disk is drive D. If your RAM disk isn't drive D, use its drive letter instead of D.) The output of the Chkdsk command will look similar to this:

```
Volume MS-RAMDRIVE created 07-21-1992 12:00a

   62464 bytes total disk space
   62464 bytes available on disk

     512 bytes in each allocation unit
     122 total allocation units on disk
     122 available allocation units on disk

  655360 total bytes memory
  635648 bytes free
```

Note: *The memory information provided by the Chkdsk command is limited to conventional memory. To obtain information about expanded and extended memory as well, use the Mem command.*

A 64-KB RAM disk isn't useful for much (although a 16-KB RAM disk is wonderful for storing batch files—more on that later). For best performance, you should specify a RAM disk as large as the amount of free extended or expanded memory on your computer, up to 4 MB or however much memory you can spare (without taking memory away from programs that can make better use of it). A good size for everyone, however, is a 512-KB RAM disk. The command to create a 512-KB RAM disk in extended memory is

```
device=c:\dos\ramdrive.sys 512 /e
```

Loading RAMDRIVE.SYS High

Because you've learned to be a conscientious MS-DOS memory user, you're probably wondering how much of your precious conventional memory the RAMDRIVE.SYS device driver is using. Rest assured, the RAMDRIVE.SYS device driver only eats a paltry 1 KB of conventional memory. This can be confirmed using the Mem /m command:

```
C:\>mem /m ramdrive

RAMDRIVE is using the following memory:

Segment  Region     Total         Type
-------  ------  ----------------  --------
 00253           1184     (1K)  Installed Device=RAMDRIVE
                 ----------------
Total Size:      1184     (1K)
```

Even though RAMDRIVE.SYS only nibbles at conventional memory, it's still possible—and highly recommended—to load its 1184 bytes of RAM into upper memory.

Note: When you load the RAMDRIVE.SYS device driver into a UMB, you load only the device driver—not the RAM disk itself, which can be in conventional, extended, or expanded memory. Also, no matter how many RAM disks you create or how big the RAM disks are, each RAMDRIVE.SYS device driver takes up just over 1 KB of memory.

To load the RAMDRIVE.SYS device driver into a UMB, use the following command in your CONFIG.SYS file:

```
devicehigh=c:\dos\ramdrive.sys
```

Of course, indicate the proper path (C:\DOS is assumed above), and add whatever switches you need (/e to use extended memory; /a to use expanded memory).

Note: This is an example of how the "easy way out" strategy of using MS-DOS's MemMaker tool can be inefficient. It would take more time to load RAMDRIVE.SYS high using MemMaker than it would to simply edit your CONFIG.SYS file and change device *to* devicehigh. *Especially if you're experimenting with several RAM disks, loading RAMDRIVE.SYS manually saves time; although I do recommend running MemMaker when you have everything "just so," to ensure that as many device drivers and memory-resident programs as possible fit into upper memory.*

RAM Disk Strategy

To run an application from a RAM disk, you must first copy the application to the RAM disk. But after you've finished running the application, you must copy any new or changed data (saved on the RAM disk) back to the hard disk for permanent storage. Two simple rules cover this:

■ Copy disk-intensive applications to the RAM disk, and then run the application from the RAM disk.

■ After you've finished running the application, copy any new or changed data files (a word processor document, a spreadsheet file, program source code, and so on) from the RAM disk to the hard disk.

If you're good with MS-DOS, use batch files to copy the application to a RAM disk, and then run the application from the RAM disk. Advanced MS-DOS users typically use batch files to run most applications. Adding a few commands to copy applications to the RAM disk—and then to copy new or changed data files back to the hard disk when you've finished with the applications—takes only two more commands in the batch file.

If you're *really* good with MS-DOS, you can include the commands to copy applications to a RAM disk in your AUTOEXEC.BAT file. The drawback to this is that it can take a long time for your computer to boot. An example is provided later in this chapter.

The following sections give examples of using a RAM disk in various situations and for various purposes.

Disk-Intensive Applications

Any disk-intensive application will run faster from a RAM disk. The problem is really one of space. For example, if you have 4 MB of extra memory in your PC—enough to run most disk-intensive applications—would that memory be better used elsewhere?

If the disk-intensive application doesn't occupy too much disk space, and you have the RAM to spare, consider moving the application to a RAM disk. First you need to add a command to your CONFIG.SYS file to create a RAM disk (if you haven't already created a RAM disk). Suppose that your application and its support files require 2 MB of storage space. Use the MS-DOS Edit program to add the following command (or modify the command that creates your RAM disk) to your CONFIG.SYS file:

```
devicehigh=c:\dos\ramdrive.sys 2048 /e
```

This command creates a 2-MB RAM disk in extended memory (the /a switch would create the RAM disk in expanded memory) and assumes that RAMDRIVE.SYS is in the C:\DOS subdirectory. If RAMDRIVE.SYS is not in the C:\DOS subdirectory, specify the correct path.

Save your CONFIG.SYS file, and reboot your computer. Watch for the RAMDRIVE.SYS startup message to determine which drive letter MS-DOS assigns to the RAM disk.

Now you need to add commands to your AUTOEXEC.BAT file that copy your disk-intensive application to your RAM disk. Use the MS-DOS Edit program to add these commands to the end of your AUTOEXEC.BAT file:

```
md d:\word
xcopy c:\word\*.* d:\word /s
```

Things to Do with a RAM Disk

I once read with great enthusiasm a magazine article that purportedly gave away speed-boosting secrets for 100 MS-DOS applications. Allow me to summarize it for you: *Use a RAM disk.* For applications that couldn't benefit from a RAM disk, the author had the following suggestion: *Add expanded memory.* (And they paid this guy!)

A RAM disk is most helpful with the following types of programs:

- **Applications that frequently access a disk drive.** Any disk-intensive program will benefit from a RAM disk. (A compiler is a good example.) If the hard-disk light frequently flashes while an application is running, copy the entire application to a RAM disk, and run the application from the RAM disk. (You'll see how to do this later in this chapter.)

- **Applications with overlay files.** Many applications are too big to fit into conventional memory. One common solution to this problem is to break up an application into several smaller modules called *overlays*. Each overlay contains instructions that handle a specific task. For example, a word processor might have an overlay for saving and loading documents, an overlay for checking spelling, an overlay for printing, and so on.

The word processor has a main unit that always stays in memory. This unit handles ordinary tasks—inserting and deleting text, cutting and pasting, and so on. But when you do something special—like printing—the main unit must load the printing overlay from disk and transfer control to the printing overlay.

This example makes two assumptions. The first assumption is that your RAM disk is drive D. If your RAM disk is not drive D, specify the proper drive letter instead. The second assumption is that the application you're copying is in the C:\WORD subdirectory. On your system, specify the correct path.

The printing overlay performs the print operation, exits (freeing the memory it was using), and returns control to the word processor's main unit.

This solution has one disadvantage: The delay that occurs while an overlay loads from disk can be annoying. That's why running this type of application from a RAM disk is such an improvement. Overlay files load much faster from a RAM disk than from an actual disk drive.

- **Graphics applications.** Sometimes large graphics images can't be stored in memory all at once. Some graphics applications will save and load pieces of the image on disk as you manipulate the image. If your graphics application will load and save these pieces on a RAM disk, the application will work faster with large images.

A RAM disk isn't helpful for the following types of programs and situations:

- **Applications that rarely access a disk.** RAM disks are beneficial only to programs that load or save information on disk.

- **Copy-protected software.** Although few applications are copy protected anymore, those that are probably won't run from a RAM disk. (This category includes computer games, which tend to be copy protected more than other applications.)

- **Power failures.** When the power goes off, any information on the RAM disk is lost.

You might also need to place the application's files in your computer's search path. Add the subdirectory on the RAM disk to your Path command in AUTOEXEC.BAT.

Save AUTOEXEC.BAT, and reboot your computer. After the computer boots, run your disk-intensive application to ensure that it works. If you're successful, you'll be amazed at the increased speed the program offers—and the dead silence from your hard disk. Be sure to copy any files or documents created on the RAM disk back to the hard disk when you exit your disk-intensive application.

Temporary and Overflow Files

Some applications use a subdirectory for temporary or overflow files. For example, both MS-DOS and Microsoft Windows let you specify a directory for temporary files using the environment variable TEMP. Why not specify the root directory of your RAM disk? You'll notice a significant speed increase while running Windows. (More hints on optimizing Windows' performance are given in the next chapter.)

Ventura Publisher and other large applications that work with lots of data let you specify a RAM disk for overflow files. WordPerfect's Setup command tells WordPerfect where to save temporary and timed backup files, so why not use a RAM disk for these files? You can copy the spelling and thesaurus files to a RAM disk and then use WordPerfect's Setup command to tell WordPerfect to look for the spelling and thesaurus files on the RAM disk. You can perform a spelling check much faster when the dictionary is on a RAM disk.

Many applications have a command that tells the application where to store temporary and overflow files. For optimal performance, create a RAM disk, at least 1 MB in size, specifically for these temporary files.

Optimizing for Batch Files

Anyone who uses MS-DOS should consider batch files as a productivity booster. On my computer, *all* applications are run through batch files, which are all located on a RAM disk. The batch files are all created and stored in the BATCH subdirectory on the hard disk. When my computer boots, my AUTOEXEC.BAT file copies the batch files to the RAM disk, and then places the RAM disk on the search path. The following lines in AUTOEXEC.BAT do the job:

```
xcopy c:\batch\*.* d:\
path=d:\;c:\dos;c:\util
```

If you want to *really* maximize performance, create a unique RAM disk for your batch files. Make the RAM disk small and the sector size small, because batch files don't require much space. (A small sector size is most efficient for small files.) But specify quite a few directory entries in the root directory of the RAM disk. Inserting the following command in your CONFIG.SYS file would work well:

```
devicehigh=c:\dos\ramdrive.sys 16 128 128 /e
```

This command creates a 16-KB RAM disk in extended memory with 128-byte sectors and room for 128 directory entries in the root directory. Add a command to your AUTOEXEC.BAT file to copy all your batch files from the hard disk to the RAM disk, and then add the RAM disk to your computer's search path.

It's important to remember that the batch files are on the RAM disk. If you add or edit a batch file, do so on the hard disk, and then copy the new batch file to your RAM disk. (Otherwise the new batch file or change will be lost when you turn off the computer.)

The Download Directory

If you use your computer for telecommunications, you can *download* software from national on-line networks, local computers, or the office. If so, using a RAM disk as the download directory saves time. Additionally, because most downloaded software is in a compressed format, decompressing the files on the RAM disk will go faster as well.

Demo Programs

In the same vein as downloading programs, it pays sometimes to install demo software on a RAM disk. Run the program from the RAM disk. If you like the program, copy it to a subdirectory on your hard disk. If you don't like the program, it will automatically be discarded when you turn off your computer. The only drawback occurs if a demo insists on reboot-ing your computer to run itself. When that happens, the RAM disk is erased, and the demo is gone.

USING A DISK CACHE

Disk caches and RAM disks are almost always mentioned in the same breath. True, both take advantage of memory to improve your computer's performance. But that's where the similarity ends.

A disk cache (pronounced *cash*) is basically a large disk buffer, a storage place in memory for information read from disk. When MS-DOS reads in-formation from disk, a copy of the information is kept in the cache, from which it can be quickly read again, as necessary. Reading the information from the disk cache is much faster than reading it from disk.

Using the SMARTDrive Disk Cache

The disk cache that comes with MS-DOS is called SMARTDrive. SMARTDrive was designed for use with Microsoft Windows, but even-tually migrated to MS-DOS in version 5 as SMARTDRV.SYS, and was in-stalled using a device command in CONFIG.SYS. With MS-DOS 6, SMARTDrive is a memory-resident program, and is installed using a com-mand in AUTOEXEC.BAT.

SMARTDrive offers both read caching and write caching of your disk drives. Read caching works as described in the previous section: Informa-tion read from disk is stored in memory for quick retrieval. Write caching works by holding information to be written to disk in a cache, and then writing several groups of information to disk in a single operation instead of writing one group at a time. Notice that this can be a problem: If you turn off the computer before the information is written to disk, the infor-mation is lost. See the next section, "Creating the Disk Cache," to learn how to disable write caching.

SMARTDrive uses the following, basic format. (The full format is shown in Appendix B.)

```
c:\dos\smartdrv.exe [[drive[+¦-]]...]
```

Be sure to specify the proper path; in this example, the C:\DOS subdirectory is assumed. You don't need to specify the subdirectory if it's on your computer's search path.

drive is the letter of the disk drive you want cached; only the drive letter is specified, no colon. *drive* is optional because SMARTDrive automatically caches all your floppy drives and hard disks. To activate both read and write caching, specify a plus sign (+) after the drive letter. To deactivate caching on a specific drive, specify a minus sign (−) after the drive letter. And to activate only read caching on a disk drive, specify only its letter.

Note: Unlike the old version of SMARTDrive, SMARTDRV.SYS, the size of the default cache created by the new version is based on the total amount of available extended memory. See Appendix B for the exact figures for the size of the default cache.

Creating the Disk Cache

To put SMARTDrive to work, edit AUTOEXEC.BAT and add this line:

```
c:\dos\smartdrv /v
```

Specify the proper path for SMARTDRV.EXE. (This example assumes SMARTDRV.EXE is in the C:\DOS subdirectory.) The /v switch tells SMARTDRV.EXE to display status and error messages when loading. You can remove the /v switch when you're sure SMARTDRV.EXE is loading correctly.

This is about all you need to establish a disk cache on your PC. (Older versions of SMARTDrive had you specifying a minimum and maximum cache size for use under Windows. You can still specify those values, but the values that are automatically calculated with the MS-DOS 6 version of SMARTDrive are usually sufficient. See Appendix B for the complete SMARTDrive syntax.)

Note: There is no need to load SMARTDrive high. The SMARTDRV.EXE program automatically detects UMBs and will load itself high if there's room.

Save AUTOEXEC.BAT, exit to MS-DOS, and reboot your computer.

When the computer boots, you'll see the SMARTDrive startup message, as shown at the top of the next page.

```
Microsoft SMARTDrive Disk Cache version 4.1
Copyright 1991,1993 Microsoft Corp.

Cache size: 2,097,152 bytes
Cache size while running Windows: 2,097,152 bytes

                Disk Caching Status
drive   read cache   write cache   buffering
---------------------------------------------
  A:       yes          no            no
  B:       yes          no            no
  C:       yes          yes           no

For help, type "Smartdrv /?".

The memory-resident portion of SMARTDrive is loaded.
```

Automatically, SMARTDrive has created a 2-MB cache. Drives A and B are read-cached, drive C is both read-cached and write-cached, and SMARTDrive has been loaded into a UMB. You can type *mem /m smartdrv* to confirm this.

You can type *smartdrv* at any command prompt to check on the cache's status. You will see a display similar to that shown above. You might want to try some of SMARTDrive's switches and options to customize the display or control the cache. (Be sure to exit Windows before trying these switches and options.) For example:

```
smartdrv /s
```

The output from the above command displays additional information about the cache. The *cache hits* value indicates the number of times information has been read from the cache instead of from disk. The *cache misses* value tells you how many times the disk drive truly had to be accessed. The ratio of the two numbers (cache hits divided by cache misses) gives you an estimate of how much more performance SMARTDrive is eking out of your disk system.

Type *smartdrv /c* to direct SMARTDrive to empty its write cache, saving all write-cached information in the cache to disk. This is a good command to use right before you shut off your PC.

Type *smartdrv /r* to direct SMARTDrive to restart. The cache is cleared, and SMARTDrive starts over in the same way as if it were first loaded into memory.

The Fastopen Command

MS-DOS 3.3 came with a file-location caching program called Fastopen. The first time you accessed a file, MS-DOS would look for the subdirectory that contained the file and then search that subdirectory. Using the Fastopen command, MS-DOS would keep track (in memory) of the locations of files and subdirectories you accessed. Any additional access to those files and subdirectories was much quicker because MS-DOS wouldn't need to search for the location of the file or subdirectory.

The problem with Fastopen is that it's incompatible with several hard-disk utilities. (The Norton Utilities' manual states that you shouldn't use Fastopen under any circumstance.) My advice is to dispense with Fastopen and use SMARTDrive instead. Check your CONFIG.SYS and AUTOEXEC.BAT files to ensure that the Fastopen command is not loaded.

SMARTDrive's Double Buffering Option

You might need to activate SMARTDrive's double buffering option on some hard-disk systems, particularly SCSI and some ESDI drives. (Double buffering provides compatibility for hard-disk controllers that can't work with memory provided by EMM386.EXE or that have problems with Windows' 386 enhanced mode. The MS-DOS 6 Setup program might install this option for you.) This option directs SMARTDrive to load part of itself as a device driver in CONFIG.SYS using the following command:

```
device=c:\dos\smartdrv.exe /double_buffer
```

To see if your system requires double buffering, edit CONFIG.SYS using the MS-DOS Edit program and insert the above line at the end of the file. Exit to MS-DOS and reboot your computer.

At the command prompt, type *smartdrv*. Look at the display in the buffering column. If you see "yes" anywhere in that column, your hard disk requires double buffering. If every entry in that column is "no," you can remove the *device=c:\dos\smartdrv.exe /double_buffer* line from your CONFIG.SYS file.

OTHER OPTIMIZATION HINTS

If getting your computer to run as fast as possible has become your obsession, take advantage of the following hints. Not every hint involves memory, but each one contributes to your computer's efficiency.

■ **Perform regular cleanup and file maintenance.** It's always a good idea to remove unneeded or temporary files from your hard disk. A good disk utility can help in this regard.

■ **Clean up unallocated clusters on the hard disk.** Exit Windows (if necessary) and type *chkdsk /f* at the command prompt. (Never run Chkdsk while Windows is running.) The Chkdsk command, with its /f switch, looks for lost chains and clusters on disk. Those are file fragments typically left behind when a file wasn't closed properly. This can happen when you turn off the computer without exiting an application (or when a power failure occurs). The Chkdsk command will remove these fragments, making your disk more efficient.

■ **Compress your hard disk with DeFrag.** Over time, files stored on disk tend to become broken into pieces and scattered all over the disk. (These are known as *fragmented files*.) Fragmented files take longer to load because the read/write head must be moved to read each fragment of the file.

MS-DOS's DeFrag utility will reassemble fragmented files, "gluing" them back into contiguous chunks. (Be sure to exit Windows before running DeFrag.) I have two recommendations for using DeFrag: First, only compress your hard disk if DeFrag reports that *less than* 90 percent of the drive is not fragmented (in other words, if you have more than 10 percent fragmented files). Second, specify the /B switch so that DeFrag reboots your PC after it's finished compressing your hard disk. This prevents conflicts that might occur if you're using Fastopen or the SMARTDrive disk cache.

■ **Set up a print buffer or spooler.** A *print buffer* is an area of memory used to temporarily store a file you send to the printer. The computer sends the file to the printer while letting you run an application. Although this doesn't speed up the printer, it does allow you to proceed with other activities while the file is being printed.

A *print spooler* is a program that saves (on disk) files to be printed and then prints the files while you run another application. Both the print buffer and the print spooler require special software and some unused memory. The drawback is that some buffers and spoolers are incompatible with other applications (especially applications that ignore the standard MS-DOS printing functions).

DOUBLESPACE RAM DISKS

It's possible to boost the size of your RAM disks using MS-DOS 6's disk-compression utility, DoubleSpace. To do so, follow these steps:

1. Create a RAM disk larger than 650 KB. DoubleSpace cannot compress RAM disks smaller than 650 KB.

2. At the command prompt, use the following DBLSPACE command to compress the RAM disk:

   ```
   dblspace /compress drive: /reserve=.13
   ```

   drive is the RAM disk's drive letter. If you haven't previously created a compressed drive, DoubleSpace will modify CONFIG.SYS and AUTOEXEC.BAT, and your PC will reboot one or more times.

3. After compression, type *dblspace /info* followed by the uncompressed RAM disk's drive letter. (Type *dblspace /list* to determine the uncompressed RAM disk's drive letter.) In the command's output, find the compressed RAM disk's DBLSPACE.*xxx* file and note its filename and on which drive it's stored. (As an example, I'll assume the uncompressed RAM disk is drive D and the compressed RAM disk is drive J throughout the rest of this section.)

4. Copy the the uncompressed RAM disk's DBLSPACE.xxx file from the uncompressed RAM disk to a subdirectory on your hard disk. First you'll need to remove the file's system, read-only, and hidden attributes using an Attrib command similar to the following:

   ```
   attrib -s -r -h j:\dblspace.000
   ```

   Then copy the file to a subdirectory on your hard disk for storage:

   ```
   copy j:\dblspace.000 c:\temp
   ```

5. To recreate and mount the DoubleSpace RAM disk when your computer starts again, place these three commands in AUTOEXEC.BAT:

```
copy c:\temp\dblspace.000 d:
attrib +s +r +h d:\dblspace.000
dblspace /mount d:
```

The first command copies the DBLSPACE.xxx file to your uncompressed RAM disk; the second command sets the proper attributes for the file; the final command mounts the DoubleSpace RAM disk.

SUMMARY

If you have extra memory, two good ways to put it to use are as a RAM disk and as a disk cache. Both a RAM disk and a disk cache use memory to improve your PC's performance: A RAM disk operates like an very fast disk drive; and a disk cache speeds up read operations on your hard disks.

■ A RAM disk is part of your computer's memory and behaves like a disk drive. The RAMDRIVE.SYS device driver fools MS-DOS into thinking that the RAM disk is really another disk drive. Because that disk is in memory, it works much faster than a real disk drive.

■ The RAMDRIVE.SYS device driver that comes with MS-DOS lets you create a RAM disk from 4 KB through 32,767 MB in size (limited by the amount of memory in your computer) in conventional, extended, or expanded memory. You can create as many RAM disks as you like, limited by the amount of memory in your computer.

■ The RAMDRIVE.SYS device driver can be loaded into a UMB using the Devicehigh command. But note that only the device driver—not the RAM disk itself—will be loaded into a UMB.

■ You can run any disk-intensive application from a RAM disk to greatly improve the application's performance. However, if you create any new data files (or modify existing files) on the RAM disk, always copy them to the hard disk before turning off your computer.

■ A disk cache is a part of memory used to store information read from disk. When that information needs to be read again, it's read from the disk cache instead of from disk. The end result is a faster PC.

■ The disk cache that comes with MS-DOS is SMARTDrive. It automatically creates a disk cache for all floppy and hard disks in your system. This will improve disk performance on all hard disks.

Chapter 8

Preparing for Microsoft Windows

Microsoft Windows is pretty to look at, fun to use, gives your PC graphics muscle, and exploits the full power of your machine.

It also requires a lot of memory.

MS-DOS is now tailored to work well with Windows, giving you much more free conventional memory for your applications.

In this chapter, you'll learn how to use MS-DOS to make Windows run more efficiently. You'll also benefit from specific tips that help you get the most from Windows. Most of these suggestions work best if you're running Windows on a '386-based computer that has 2 MB (or more) of extended memory, although many of the suggestions here will help 80286-based computers, even when they're not running Windows.

USING MS-DOS AND WINDOWS

Microsoft Windows 3.1 has two modes of operation: *386 enhanced mode* for '386-based computers with at least 2 MB of extended memory, and *standard mode* for 80286-based computers. Although '386-based computers can run Windows in the lesser, standard mode, you usually want to run Windows in the most powerful mode possible for your PC. This means that your computer needs plenty of extended memory available, plus as much free conventional memory as possible.

Note: Windows 3.0 had a third mode, the real *mode. It was available to 8088/8086 PCs and other systems without enough memory. Starting with version 3.1, Windows no longer has a real mode.*

123

Setting Up Memory

The first concern is extended memory: Windows wants a lot of it. You need at least 384 KB of extended memory on an 80286-based or a '386-based PC to run Windows in standard mode; and you need 1 MB of extended memory (2 MB total memory) on a '386-compatible PC to run Windows in enhanced mode. Windows doesn't use expanded memory.

When you run the Windows Setup program, it automatically installs the HIMEM.SYS device driver in the CONFIG.SYS file on 80286-based or '386-based computers:

```
device =c:\windows\himem.sys
```

Coincidentally, that's also the first step required for MS-DOS to get the most from memory: HIMEM.SYS manages the use of extended memory. Furthermore, HIMEM.SYS gives 80286-based and '386-based computers access to the high memory area (HMA).

Note: The HMA is most useful as a storage area for part of MS-DOS. (See Chapter 5.)

If your CONFIG.SYS file contains expanded memory manager device drivers, Windows won't choke. Some of your MS-DOS applications that run under Windows in 386 enhanced mode might require expanded memory. If so, you must prepare the expanded memory in the same way as you would when running MS-DOS without Windows. However, all that expanded memory you create is extended memory that's not available for Windows. My advice: Look for a Windows-based application to replace your MS-DOS application that needs expanded memory, and then dispense with expanded memory.

After all device drivers and memory-resident programs have been loaded into UMBs, the only extra thing you can do to get better performance from Windows is to add more extended memory to your computer. On a '386-based computer, 2 MB of memory is barely enough to run Windows in 386 enhanced mode. To get the best performance from Windows, be sure your computer has at least 4 MB of extended memory. In fact, that will give you enough memory to use a disk cache and possibly create a RAM disk. (See Chapter 7.)

Next you'll want to clear out conventional memory. (Follow the procedure described in Chapter 5.) Although Windows needs only a small amount of conventional memory to start, you want to have as much free conventional memory as possible for running your MS-DOS applications under Windows. In the olden days, Windows gave you about 536 KB of free conventional memory for MS-DOS applications. But by loading device drivers and memory-resident programs into UMBs (as described in Chapters 5 and 6), you can have up to 615 KB (or more) of free conventional memory when running Windows.

Setting Up AUTOEXEC.BAT

Now that you've structured the computer's memory to work with Windows, you can make two changes to AUTOEXEC.BAT. These changes allow AUTOEXEC.BAT to start Windows when your computer boots:

1. Add your Windows subdirectory to the Path command. (This might have already been done by the Windows Setup program.)

2. Place the Win command at the end of your AUTOEXEC.BAT file.

   Note: If you have an EGA graphics card and monitor, be sure the command device=c:\dos\ega.sys *is in your CONFIG.SYS file. Be sure to specify the correct path for EGA.SYS. It's okay to load the EGA.SYS device driver into a UMB. (Use the MSD utility to confirm that your PC has an EGA graphics card installed.)*

3. Save AUTOEXEC.BAT and then reboot your computer. Your computer will boot and then load Windows.

4. After Windows has loaded, open the Program Manager if it isn't already open. Drop down the Help menu and select the last item, About Program Manager. You will see a dialog box similar to the one shown in Figure 8-1 on the following page.

In the About Program Manager dialog box, you'll see several important items of information. First is the mode Windows is running in. In Figure 8-1, you can see that Windows is running in 386 enhanced mode on my system. Confirm that Windows is running in the mode you expected, the best mode possible on your computer.

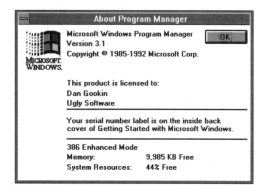

Figure 8-1. *The About Program Manager dialog box.*

If you don't see the mode you expected, you must make some adjustments. If you have a '386-based computer and have prepared it as described in Chapters 5 and 6, yet you see Real Mode or Standard Mode displayed, you should edit your CONFIG.SYS file and confirm that EMM386.EXE isn't using all of extended memory to simulate expanded memory. Also be sure you have enough extended memory installed: Windows comes up in a lesser mode when an 80286-based or a '386-based computer doesn't have enough extended memory for standard mode or 386 enhanced mode.

The amount of free memory displayed in the About Program Manager dialog box might be more memory than is in your computer. Don't panic. Windows is telling you how much conventional, extended, and *virtual* memory is available. Windows provides virtual memory by using a portion of the hard disk to simulate extra RAM.

To see how much memory is installed in your computer, use the Mem command:

1. Close the About Program Manager dialog box, and double-click the MS-DOS Prompt icon in the Main group.

2. At the MS-DOS prompt, type *mem.* You'll see something like the following:

```
Memory Type        Total =  Used  +  Free
---------------    ------   ------    ------

Conventional        640K     31K      609K
Upper               155K    155K        0K
Adapter RAM/ROM     229K    229K        0K
Extended (XMS)     2917K   3072K     1024K
---------------    ------   ------    ------

Total memory       4096K   3487K     1633K

Total under 1 MB    795K    186K      609K

Largest executable program size       609K   (623360 bytes)
Largest free upper memory block         0K        (0 bytes)
MS-DOS is resident in the high memory area.
```

Only 4 MB of RAM are installed on my computer, all of it set aside as extended memory that Windows can use. In an MS-DOS full-screen window (which is what the above output reflects), I have 623,360 bytes of unused conventional memory. That's quite a bit considering all that Windows is doing. (And that number could probably be made even larger.)

3. Type *exit* to close the full-screen MS-DOS window and return to Windows.

The WINA20.386 File

The WINA20.386 file was required when running MS-DOS 5 with Windows 3.0. If you've upgraded to Windows 3.1 (which I recommend), you no longer need WINA20.386 in your root directory; you can delete it. (You'll need to use the Attrib command to remove the read-only attribute first.) Otherwise, WINA20.386 is required on a '386-based computer to keep Windows 3.0 enhanced mode compatible with the way MS-DOS accesses the HMA.

OPTIMIZING WINDOWS' PERFORMANCE

When you're trying to optimize Windows' performance, you're simply dealing with a question of resource management. Disk storage and memory are the two main resources you can manipulate to give Windows more speed and power. Of course, you could always throw money at the problem and buy the fastest, most expensive computer with a huge, fast, hard disk and megabytes of RAM. But because, unlike the United States government, you're probably required to operate within a budget, you must make the most of what you already have.

First upgrade to MS-DOS 6, and then free as much conventional memory as possible, as described in Chapters 5 and 6. After that, your Windows optimization strategy becomes more specific, depending on your computer's resources.

The following sections list various steps you can take to get the most from Windows. Practice with several configurations and options—especially if memory is low—before creating your ideal Windows setup.

Using SMARTDrive

Under most circumstances, the MS-DOS 6 and Windows 3.1 Setup programs install the SMARTDrive disk cache in your AUTOEXEC.BAT file. This is great because Windows is a disk-intensive program, and anything that speeds up your disk operations will make Windows run faster as well.

SMARTDrive automatically allocates extended memory as a disk cache, depending on how much total memory is in your PC. Table 8-1 shows you how much memory SMARTDrive uses for its cache in Windows based on the total amount of memory in your system.

Extended memory	Cache size	Cache in Windows
up to 1 MB	All extended memory	0 KB
up to 2 MB	1 MB	256 KB
up to 4 MB	1 MB	512 KB
up to 6 MB	2 MB	1 MB
more than 6 MB	2 MB	2 MB

Table 8-1. *SMARTDrive's memory allocation.*

Table 8-1 shows that if you have a '386 system with 4 MB of memory, SMARTDrive will use 1 MB for its cache. When Windows runs on this system, it will shrink the cache size down to 512 KB, freeing the remainder for its applications. Notice that a PC with 1 MB of extended memory has a cache size of zero in Windows. In this situation Windows makes all of extended memory available instead of using a cache. (When there is little free memory, that memory is more important for Windows than it is for the cache.)

You can adjust these figures by specifying two values when you start the SMARTDrive disk cache. The first value is the initial cache size, and the second is the cache size under Windows. For example, suppose your computer has 2 MB of memory and you'd like a 512 KB cache size in Windows. You would use the following command in AUTOEXEC.BAT:

```
smartdrv 1024 512
```

The initial size of the cache, under MS-DOS, will be 1 MB. In Windows, the size will be reduced to 512 KB (as opposed to 256 KB). If you wanted all your extended memory for Windows and no cache while Windows is running, you would specify the following:

```
smartdrv 1024 0
```

The size of the cache under MS-DOS is still 1 MB, but in Windows the size would be reduced to zero. That would make the full 2 MB available for use in Windows.

Note: *The SMARTDrive disk cache is covered in detail in Chapter 7.*

Using RAMDrive

Installing any disk-intensive programs in the RAM disk boosts productivity without a doubt, particularly when you're running Windows. The drawback is that most Windows-based applications take up too much disk space to make the RAM disk effective. As a result, memory spent on a RAM disk would take away memory better put to use for Windows.

Instead of installing a Windows-based application on a RAM disk, you can use the RAM disk for storing Windows' temporary files. The RAM disk should be at least 2 MB in size, which means you need to have several megabytes of available extended memory. (I suggest doing this only on machines with at least 8 MB of RAM; systems with less memory really can't take advantage of a RAM disk.)

To set up the RAM disk, you add a command in CONFIG.SYS to load the RAMDRIVE.SYS device driver. For example, the following command in CONFIG.SYS creates a 2-MB RAM disk:

```
devicehigh=c:\dos\ramdrive.sys 2048 /e
```

The /e switch creates the RAM disk in extended memory. Refer to Chapter 7 for more information about the RAMDRIVE.SYS device driver.

After the RAM disk is created, you tell Windows to use the RAM disk for temporary files by adding the following command to your AUTOEXEC.BAT file:

```
set temp=d:\
```

This command assumes that your RAM disk is drive D. If necessary, substitute the proper drive letter for your RAM disk. MS-DOS also uses the TEMP environment variable to determine where to store its own temporary files, so using a RAM disk for temporary files improves the performance of both Windows and MS-DOS.

Note: Some programs append a backslash to the end of the TEMP environment variable. (The programs try to save temporary files using a format similar to %TEMP%\~DOC.TMP). You'll see an error message similar to Can't open temporary file *when these programs run. If you see such an error message, set the TEMP variable to D: instead of D:\ in your AUTOEXEC.BAT file, exit any running applications and Windows, and reboot your computer.*

Using the Swap File

In 386 enhanced mode, Windows can use a *swap file* (a hidden file on your hard disk) to simulate additional physical memory. (The process of using a file on your hard disk to simulate additional memory is known as *virtual memory*.) When Windows is low on memory, inactive applications are saved in the swap file, freeing memory for other applications. Essentially, Windows puts an application away on disk—in virtual memory—and loads the application back into physical memory only when needed.

Windows can use two different types of swap files: *temporary* or *permanent*. A temporary swap file exists only while Windows is running (which is useful if you don't have much free space on your hard disk). When Windows starts, it creates the temporary swap file on your computer's hard disk, and deletes the swap file when it exits.

A permanent swap file is a file on your hard disk that exists whether or not Windows is running. A permanent swap file is generally faster than a temporary swap file because it is *contiguous* (all the "pieces" of the file are located in one area on the hard disk).

To create a permanent swap file, or to confirm that Windows is using a permanent swap file, follow these steps:

1. Start Windows' Control Panel by double clicking the Control Panel icon in the Main group in Program Manager.

2. Double click the 386 Enhanced icon in the Control Panel window. You will see the 386 Enhanced dialog box for controlling Windows' 386 enhanced mode options.

3. Click the Virtual Memory button in the 386 Enhanced dialog box. In the Virtual Memory dialog box that appears, click the Change button. You will see a dialog box similar to the one shown in Figure 8-2.

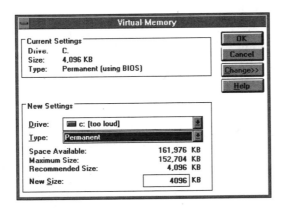

Figure 8-2. *The Virtual Memory dialog box.*

At the top of the Virtual Memory window, you'll see what type of swap file your PC has, on which drive it's located, and its size. Figure 8-2 shows a permanent swap file of 4 MB on drive C. The bottom of the Virtual Memory dialog box shows more information, including a list of drives for the swap file, a list of swap file types, the amount of free space on the selected drive, and the maximum and recommended sizes of a swap file.

If you don't have a permanent swap file, create one. Use the size Windows suggests or a smaller size if disk space is tight (or when Windows suggests a ridiculously large swap file size). Note that you cannot create a permanent swap file on a networked or compressed drive, such as those created by DoubleDisk or Stacker. I recommend everyone have at least a 2-MB permanent swap file. If you have the room, create a 4-MB file. Anything larger is a waste of disk space (unless you frequently run several large applications simultaneously in Windows).

Note: You might want to run the DeFrag utility on your hard drive before creating or changing a swap file to free up some contiguous space for a large permanent swap file. Exit Windows, run DeFrag with the /b switch (to reboot your PC afterwards), and select the full optimize method. After your system reboots, start Windows again. Now you should have plenty of room for a larger swap file.

Eliminating Unnecessary Device Drivers and Memory-Resident Programs

Windows can run just fine without the following:

- **The mouse device driver**. Windows uses its own mouse driver, so you don't need to load a mouse device driver in CONFIG.SYS or AUTOEXEC.BAT. The exception is when you run MS-DOS applications that use the mouse from MS-DOS or under Windows. If so, continue to load your mouse device driver.

- **The Doskey command line enhancer**. If you load Doskey, you can use it any time you start an MS-DOS window in Windows. If you do all your work in Windows, you can dispense with Doskey.

- **The ANSI device driver**. ANSI.SYS controls your screen and keyboard, but only under MS-DOS or an MS-DOS window in Windows. If you must run batch files that use ANSI commands in an MS-DOS window, load ANSI.SYS. Otherwise, ANSI.SYS is using 4 KB of memory Windows could use.

- **The Print program**. Print is a memory-resident print queue. Windows uses the Print Manager, so there's no need to waste memory on the Print program if you do all your work in Windows.

- **The Graphics program**. Graphics adjusts color graphics images for specific printers. This is wholly unnecessary under Windows, which has many more exciting ways to print color images. (The Graphics program might be necessary if you run MS-DOS applications under Windows or from MS-DOS.)

- **The Append program**. Append makes the files in one directory appear to be part of the current directory, which helps MS-DOS applications find files. Windows does not need Append to help it search for files. Setting a search path using the Path command is important, but the Append program isn't necessary for Windows.

Cleaning Up CONFIG.SYS

Here are some CONFIG.SYS recommendations for optimizing Windows' performance:

- Load the HIMEM.SYS device driver on 80286-based and '386-based computers to give MS-DOS access to the HMA.

- Load part of MS-DOS into the HMA on 80286-based and '386-based computers by using the Dos=high command.

- Let EMM386.EXE create UMBs on '386-based computers. Specify the noems option to do this.

- Don't load device drivers you don't need. Better still, put a REM command in front of commands that load unneeded device drivers. If you ever need to load one of these device drivers, remove the REM command, and reboot your computer.

■ Load device drivers into UMBs. Refer to the instructions in Chapter 6 for more information.

■ Use the most recent version of the EMM386.EXE device driver.

■ You should generally specify a value of 30 or less for the Files command. (Incidentally, each value greater than 8 uses about 48 bytes of conventional memory.)

■ Specify a value of 20 for the Buffers command. If you're using the SMARTDrive disk cache device driver, specify a value of 15 for the Buffers command.

■ Specify exactly how many drives you have for the Lastdrive command. Each drive you specify above drive E uses about 80 bytes of conventional memory.

■ Set the Stacks command as follows: *stacks=0,0*. By default, Stacks is set to 9,256 on 80286-based and '386-based computers. Each stack uses a lot of memory; multiply the two values in a Stacks command to see how many bytes are being used. If Windows occasionally locks up your computer, set the Stacks command to *stacks=9,256*.

Note: You might not be able to run Windows' Setup program from the command prompt if the Stacks command is stacks=0,0. *Set the Stacks command to* stacks=9,256 *before running Setup. After you run Setup, edit CONFIG.SYS, and then reset the Stacks command.*

■ Change all Install commands in CONFIG.SYS to Loadhigh commands in AUTOEXEC.BAT. The Install command loads memory-resident programs into conventional memory instead of into UMBs.

Cleaning Up AUTOEXEC.BAT

Here are some AUTOEXEC.BAT recommendations for optimizing Windows' performance:

■ Don't load unneeded memory-resident programs. In some cases, you'll find equivalent programs that run under Windows. Better still, if the program has a non-memory-resident mode, run it in its own MS-DOS window.

■ Load your necessary memory-resident programs into UMBs using the Loadhigh command. Refer to Chapter 6.

Hard-Disk Maintenance

Although many users neglect the task, routine hard-disk maintenance is a must for getting the most from your computer:

■ Delete unneeded files, and remove unused subdirectories.

■ Before running Windows, use the Chkdsk /f command to locate and remove lost clusters. (Do not use this command while Windows is running.)

■ Occasionally run DeFrag or a comparable disk defragmentation program to defragment your computer's hard disk. (Do not use this type of program while Windows is running.)

■ After running Windows, delete any Windows temporary files that remain in the root directory of your hard disk. Because these files typically begin with the -- (tilde) character, use the following command in your AUTOEXEC.BAT file:

```
if exist c:\~*.* del c:\~*.*
```

(Do not use this command while Windows is running.)

■ Back up your hard disk. MS-DOS 6 comes with a special backup program for Windows. Third-party backup programs are also available. Use them! I perform a full hard-disk backup once a month and a daily backup of all files I work on. Get into this routine! (I became a convert after losing a 90-MB hard disk, paying $1000 for a replacement (this was when hard disks were more expensive), *and* wasting three days retyping all my data. Don't make the same mistake.)

SUMMARY

Windows needn't be a drain on your PC's resources. With the proper configuration, your computer can handle Windows' demands quite easily.

■ To run in standard mode, Windows requires at least 384 KB of extended memory on 80286-based and '386-based computers. Load the HIMEM.SYS device driver to manage your computer's extended memory, and let MS-DOS access the HMA.

■ Free as much conventional memory as possible for Windows by loading part of MS-DOS into the HMA and creating UMBs. To create the UMBs without creating unneeded expanded memory, use EMM386.EXE's noems option.

■ Load your device drivers and memory-resident programs into UMBs with the Devicehigh and the Loadhigh commands. Load only those device drivers and memory-resident programs that you need.

■ Load the SMARTDrive disk cache program to improve Windows' disk-access time. Give Windows a good-sized disk cache, but devote the majority of any extra memory to a RAM disk instead.

■ Use the RAMDRIVE.SYS device driver to create a RAM disk, primarily for Windows' temporary files. If your computer has enough memory, however, use the RAM disk to store Windows-based applications or Windows program files. This typically takes a 2-MB or larger RAM disk, but the speed improvement is striking.

■ Clean up your CONFIG.SYS and AUTOEXEC.BAT files. Performing regular hard-disk maintenance is also a good idea.

Chapter 9
Using MS-DOS and Other Memory Managers

This chapter is about a few of the many products that augment and extend the memory-management capabilities of MS-DOS. The two leaders in the field of memory managers are QEMM-386 from Quarterdeck Office Systems and 386MAX from Qualitas. Another favorite is V Communications' Memory Commander. That's the program that produced the awesome 742 KB free conventional memory value you read about in the Introduction of this book.

Memory solutions for 80286-based and even older 8088/8086-based computers are also provided in this chapter. For those machines, Quarterdeck makes QRAM, which is comparable to QEMM-386, and Qualitas makes the MOVE'EM memory manager, which is now bundled with 386MAX. So don't despair; there are memory solutions for every level of PC.

MEMORY MANAGERS BEYOND MS-DOS

386MAX, QEMM-386, Memory Commander, and QRAM all offer one or more of the following features:

- An extended memory manager for computers with extended memory

- The ability to simulate expanded memory by using extended memory on a '386-based computer

- An expanded memory manager and backfilling support for 8088/8086-based and 80286-based computers with expanded memory

- The ability to load device drivers and memory-resident programs into UMBs

- The ability to load computer resources into UMBs

- The ability to "steal" video memory to get more conventional memory

Each of these products is introduced alphabetically in the following sections. The rest of this chapter provides general hints and strategies for memory management.

386MAX, BlueMAX, and MOVE'EM

Qualitas makes 386MAX for '386-based computers with at least 256 KB of extended memory. In addition to a memory manager, 386MAX comes with the ASQ memory information utility; a handy editor for CONFIG.SYS, AUTOEXEC.BAT, and the 386MAX Profile text file; its own disk cache, Qcache, which replaces MS-DOS's SMARTDrive; and a RAM disk device driver, 386DISK.

A counterpart to 386MAX is BlueMAX, which is specifically designed for IBM PS/2 '386-based computers. BlueMAX takes the Advanced BIOS in those machines and compresses it, freeing up extra UMBs. It also eliminates the seldom-used ROM BASIC in PS/2s, making even more memory available. If you have a PS/2, you should consider using BlueMAX instead of 386MAX. Otherwise, the two packages function identically. (And both are referred to as *386MAX* in this chapter.)

If you have an 8088/8086-based or 80286-based computer and are jealous of what MS-DOS can do for '386-based computers, you'll be happy to know that 386MAX includes the MOVE'EM program, formerly sold separately. MOVE'EM fully addresses the desperate needs of 8088/8086 and 80286 MS-DOS users hungry for a memory manager. To use MOVE'EM, your system must be equipped with LIM EMS 4.0 hardware-compatible memory. If your computer has the NEAT, AT/386, or LEAP CHIPSet from Chips and Technologies installed, it also qualifies as MOVE'EM compatible. (Refer to your PC's manual to see whether your PC contains the required hardware.)

Memory Commander

Memory Commander from V Communications is a painlessly simple memory manager. Of everything I've seen, this product gives you the most conventional memory for MS-DOS and Microsoft Windows, plus it loads device drivers and memory-resident programs into UMBs without junking up CONFIG.SYS or AUTOEXEC.BAT. It's almost miraculous.

Unlike 386MAX and QEMM-386, Memory Commander lacks a "little brother" for 80286 and lesser machines. It also lacks the fancy utilities of the other two giants. But Memory Commander makes its mark using video memory to supplement conventional memory. By properly juggling the contents of upper memory, you can conceivably see a total of 904 KB of available conventional memory. Cough! Choke! Gag!

You can't run Windows in the 904 KB conventional memory mode, or anything more complicated than a full screen of color text (graphics are not possible in this mode). And although I tried, I could get only 742 KB available conventional memory on my system. That's still a lot of conventional memory and, when combined with the program's reticent approach to memory management, makes Memory Commander worth a peek.

QEMM-386

QEMM-386 is Quarterdeck's expanded memory manager for '386-based computers with at least 1 MB of memory. It's XMS-compatible, so it replaces HIMEM.SYS. It offers expanded memory and UMB support, so it also replaces MS-DOS's EMM386.EXE device driver. QEMM-386 also provides support for the VCPI (Virtual Control Program Interface) standard (a specification for writing MS-DOS programs that run in 80286 protected mode, 80386 protected mode, or 80386 virtual 8086 mode) for providing memory to *extended DOS* applications.

As part of the QEMM package, you also receive Quarterdeck's Manifest, a computer information program that tells you what's in your computer (both hardware and software) and how your computer's resources are being used.

QRAM

Quarterdeck's memory manager for 8088/8086-based and 80286-based computers is QRAM (pronounced *cram*). QRAM provides extended memory-management capabilities for 80286-based computers, as well as expanded memory-management capabilities for all computers equipped with EMS 4.0-compatible expanded memory. As it is with QEMM-386, Manifest is part of the QRAM package.

How This Chapter Works

Things could get messy here. Consider our subject: MS-DOS, plus several different memory-management programs for three generations of micro-processors, on computers that might or might not run Windows, plus many other nasty combinations. The mess potential waxes thick.

Read through the sections that follow, find the information that pertains to your memory manager, and then use the information along with your memory manager's manual.

INSTALLATION AND OPTIMIZATION

If you have already installed a memory manager prior to your MS-DOS upgrade, skip to the section in this chapter titled ''Basic Memory Strategy,'' which describes how to properly mix MS-DOS and third-party commands to get the most from your computer.

If you are installing a third-party memory manager on your computer, fol-low these steps:

1. Edit your CONFIG.SYS and AUTOEXEC.BAT files to remove any Devicehigh or Loadhigh commands: In CONFIG.SYS, change De-vicehigh back to Device (and remove any size parameters); in AUTOEXEC.BAT, remove Loadhigh or LH from commands that load memory-resident programs.

2. On '386-based computers, remove the command that loads the HIMEM.SYS and EMM386.EXE device drivers from CONFIG.SYS. On 8088/8086-based computers, put the command that loads your ex-panded memory manager device driver on the first line of your

CONFIG.SYS (or immediately after any commands that load hard-disk device drivers). On 80286-based computers, put the command that loads HIMEM.SYS on the first line of CONFIG.SYS, and the command that loads your expanded memory manager device driver on the second line.

3. Install the third-party memory manager according to its instructions. For now, select all the default options. (Answer *yes* to all the questions.) And be sure to *maximize* or *optimize* your computer when asked.

Note: For 386MAX, pay careful attention to the information about Windows. If you're using Windows or plan to install it in the future, be sure to answer yes *to the question about installing the Windows options.*

After the third-party memory manager is installed, your computer might reboot—maybe several times. If your computer does reboot, some of the MS-DOS commands you already installed might produce errors. That's okay for now; you'll learn how to correct this problem later in this chapter.

Note: Even with all the optimization done by the installation programs, you might still need to do some fine tuning: directing a third-party memory manager to include or exclude parts of memory, adding switches, configuring the memory manager for Windows, and so on. If your computer won't load Windows, refer to your memory manager's manual for additional fine-tuning instructions.

Assessing Installation

In the examples that follow, each third-party memory manager was installed with the following CONFIG.SYS and AUTOEXEC.BAT files. (These files might be different for 8088/8086- and 80286-based computers.)

Standard CONFIG.SYS:

```
device=c:\dos\himem.sys
dos=high
files=30
buffers=15
shell=c:\dos\command.com c:\dos\  /p
stacks=0,0
device=c:\dos\setver.exe
device=c:\dos\ramdrive.sys 512 /e
device=c:\dos\ansi.sys
```

Standard AUTOEXEC.BAT:

```
@echo off
prompt $p$g
path c:\dos;c:\util; c:\mouse
set temp=c:\temp
smartdrv
mouse
doskey /insert
```

Each installation program will modify these files as necessary and will produce a final report on the memory totals for each configuration. The output of the Mem command on my test machine that is configured with the above startup files looks like this:

```
Memory Type      Total = Used  + Free
----------------   ------   ------   ------

Conventional      640K      70K      570K
Upper               0K       0K        0K
Adapter RAM/ROM   384K     384K        0K
Extended (XMS)   3072K    1600K     1472K
----------------   ------   ------   ------
Total memory     4096K    2054K     2042K

Total under 1 MB  640K      70K      570K

Largest executable program size       570K  (584048 bytes)
Largest free upper memory block         0K      (0 bytes)
MS-DOS is resident in the high memory area.
```

A total of 570 KB conventional memory is available. (Of course, this is without MS-DOS's memory-management tools being set up properly. When that's the case, the total of free conventional memory rises to 621 KB [635,776 bytes].)

Note: Because HIMEM.SYS is incompatible with 8088/8086-based computers, owners of such computers should remove HIMEM.SYS from their CONFIG.SYS files before proceeding.

386MAX

After running the 386MAX Install program, you'll be asked if you want to maximize your computer. The Maximize program, which can also be run at the command prompt, evaluates your device drivers and memory-resident programs and then loads them into UMBs in their optimum configurations. (Be sure to remove the Install disk from drive A before running

Maximize.) If you add another device driver or memory-resident program to your computer, simply run the Maximize program again. It's easy.

Providing you chose the preselected answers to the questions asked by the Maximize program, 386MAX changes CONFIG.SYS in the following ways. Notice that new lines and changes are displayed in *italics*. (Below, the eighth and ninth lines are actually one line and should be entered as such.)

```
Device=c:\386max\386max.sys pro=c:\386max\386max.pro
dos=high
files=30
buffers=15
shell=c:\dos\command.com c:\dos\ /p
stacks=0,0
device=C:\386MAX\386load.sys size=11504 prgreg=3 prog=c:\dos\setver.exe
device=C:\386MAX\386load.sys size=5888 prgreg=3
 prog=c:\dos\ramdrive.sys 512 /e
device=C:\386MAX\386load.sys size=9072 prgreg=3 prog=c:\dos\ansi.sys
```

Above, 386MAX has first installed a command that loads itself as the memory manager for your computer. When 386MAX loads, it reads a profile report it generated when optimizing your computer. The profile, 386MAX.PRO, contains settings that tell 386MAX how to load device drivers and memory-resident software for the best overall performance.

Device drivers are loaded high using the 386LOAD.SYS program. This program specifies the device driver's size and then the name of the device driver after the *prog=* switch. This lengthens the lines in CONFIG.SYS that load device drivers, but because the Maximize program does the work, it's not a big deal.

386MAX changes AUTOEXEC.BAT in the following ways. New lines and changes are in *italics*.

```
@echo off
prompt $p$g
path c:\dos;c:\util;c:\mouse
set temp=c:\temp
C:\386MAX\386load size=41824 flexframe prog=smartdrv
C:\386MAX\386load size=56928 flexframe prog=mouse
C:\386MAX\386load size=6400 flexframe prog=doskey /insert
```

386MAX uses 386LOAD.COM to load memory-resident programs into UMBs. The Maximize program has added all the proper switches to load SMARTDrive, the Mouse device driver, and Doskey into UMBs.

Note: Even more upper memory can be made available using 386MAX's ROM Search option. If you selected the default answers when running Maximize, you skipped over the ROM Search option. To create more UMBs and load more device drivers and memory-resident programs high, rerun Maximize and specify the ROM Search option.

386MAX and MOVE'EM

MOVE'EM is installed in place of 386MAX on 80286-based and 8088/8086-based computers with EMS memory or special circuitry built into the motherboard. (You can also force MOVE'EM to install by running the Install program with the /2 switch.)

After you install MOVE'EM, you run the Maximize program, which performs the same tasks as it does for 386MAX: examining your device drivers and memory-resident programs and then loading them into UMBs. Several of the advanced Maximize options are unavailable, but other than that, the program works the same (again, providing you have the proper hardware in your PC).

The following CONFIG.SYS file displays the result of MOVE'EM's efforts on a specific 80286-based machine:

```
device=c:\dos\himem.sys
device=c:\emm.sys at 258
device=c:\move'em\move'em.mgr
dos=high
files=30
buffers=20
shell=c:\dos\command.com c:\dos\  /p
stacks=0,0
device=c:\move'em\move'em.sys prog=c:\mouse\mouse.sys /c1
```

MS-DOS's HIMEM.SYS comes first, followed by the EMM (Expanded Memory Manager) that runs the system's LIM 4.0-compatible EMS hardware. That's followed by MOVE'EM.MGR, MOVE'EM's memory manager. (MOVE'EM.SYS loads device drivers into UMBs.)

Note: If you use MOVE'EM on an 8088/8086-based computer, you should remove the dos=high *command and the command that loads the HIMEM.SYS device driver. An 8088/8086-based computer has no extended memory and therefore cannot support an HMA.*

Here is an AUTOEXEC.BAT file modified by MOVE'EM:

```
@echo off
prompt $p$g
path c:\dos;c:\util;c:\mouse
set temp=c:\temp
c:\move'em\move'em.com size=6208 prog=doskey /insert
```

MOVE'EM.COM is used to load memory-resident programs, such as Doskey, into UMBs.

Memory Commander

After a graphics check, Memory Commander installs itself onto your hard disk and updates your CONFIG.SYS and AUTOEXEC.BAT files. There are no bonus files or utilities; everything is controlled through the MC program after Memory Commander has loaded its device driver into your CONFIG.SYS file. And unlike the other memory managers, you must manually reboot your PC to continue the setup process.

Note: Older versions of Memory Commander require you to use the SetVer command to work with MS-DOS 6. (Current versions of Memory Commander will not require the SetVer command.)

Memory Commander maintains information about your system in configuration files located in your C:\MC subdirectory (where Memory Commander is installed). Very little information appears in CONFIG.SYS, although Memory Commander does do a good job of reordering commands so that device drivers are installed into UMBs as efficiently as possible.

Here's how Memory Commander changed the sample CONFIG.SYS file. New lines and changes are in *italics*.

```
break = off
buffers = 15
files = 30
stacks = 0,0
dos = high
device = C:\MC\MC.SYS
rem device=c:\dos\himem.sys
shell=c:\dos\command.com c:\dos\ /p
device=c:\dos\setver.exe
device=c:\dos\ramdrive.sys 512 /e
rem device=c:\dos\ansi.sys
```

The break=off command is inserted, as are two Rem statements. The first Rem statement disables HIMEM.SYS, which has been moved from top position to below the Memory Commander device driver, MC.SYS. The other Rem statement disables the ANSI.SYS device driver; Memory Commander supplies its own ANSI device driver. (This device driver is required to maintain compatibility because Memory Commander might move video memory.)

You might notice a lack of adulteration to the Device configuration commands—especially when compared with the other memory managers. It makes you wonder what Memory Commander is doing. The same observation can be made from AUTOEXEC.BAT as follows. New lines and changes are in *italics*.

```
@echo off
prompt $p$g
path c:\dos;c:\util;c:\mouse
set temp=c:\temp
smartdrv
mouse
doskey /insert

c:\mc\mca.exe auto optimize
```

The key is the final line—the MCA.EXE program, the Application Manager. It's a database describing your device drivers and memory-resident programs, and how and where they can be loaded in memory. In AUTOEXEC.BAT, MCA.EXE tells Memory Commander where to move your device drivers and memory-resident programs. At the command prompt, you can run MCA to customize the way the device drivers and memory-resident programs are loaded.

The MC.EXE program configures Memory Commander at the command prompt. You can select a list of memory configurations, each of which can show you different degrees of graphics ability versus total conventional memory available. Theoretically, the upper limit is 904 KB, although the most I was able to wrangle on my machine was 742 KB.

QEMM-386

QEMM-386's Install program copies all QEMM-386's programs (and the Manifest program) to your hard disk. Because you answered *yes* to all the questions, the QEMM-386 installation program has removed the command in CONFIG.SYS that loads HIMEM.SYS and replaced it with a command that loads the QEMM386.SYS device driver. It's also added the QEMM subdirectory to the search path in your AUTOEXEC.BAT file. So far, so good.

The last step performed by the install program is to run QEMM-386's Optimize program. (If not, type *optimize* at the command prompt.) Optimize works a lot like MS-DOS's MemMaker program, properly configuring your computer to load device drivers and memory-resident programs into UMBs. Follow the instructions shown on the screen. Your computer will reboot several times. Return here when you've finished.

The Optimize program evaluates your computer, the device drivers loaded by CONFIG.SYS, and the memory-resident programs loaded by AUTOEXEC.BAT. Optimize then configures QEMM-386 to load your device drivers and memory-resident programs into UMBs, taking care of all the options for you.

Optimize changes the two sample files as follows. New lines and changes are noted in *italics*.

QEMM-386's CONFIG.SYS file looks like this:

```
DEVICE=C:\QEMM\QEMM386.SYS RAM
dos=high
files=30
buffers=15
shell=c:\dos\command.com c:\dos\ /p
stacks=0,0
DEVICE=c:\qemm\loadhi.sys /r:1 c:\dos\setver.exe
DEVICE=c:\qemm\loadhi.sys /r:3 c:\dos\ramdrive.sys 512 /e
DEVICE=c:\qemm\loadhi.sys /r:1 c:\dos\ansi.sys
```

The QEMM386.SYS device driver loads first, managing your expanded and extended memory and giving MS-DOS access to the HMA.

All the device drivers are loaded into UMBs by means of the LOADHI.SYS device driver. This works a lot like MS-DOS's Devicehigh command, but because LOADHI.SYS isn't an internal MS-DOS command, the device driver's full path must be specified. The lines in CONFIG.SYS will be a bit longer because of this.

Optimize changes AUTOEXEC.BAT as follows. New lines and changes are noted in *italics*.

```
@echo off
prompt $p$g
path c:\qemm;c:\dos;c:\util;c:\mouse
set temp=c:\temp
c:\qemm\loadhi /r:2 smartdrv
c:\qemm\loadhi /r:2 mouse
c:\qemm\loadhi /r:3 doskey /insert
```

QEMM-386 uses the LOADHI.COM program to load memory-resident programs into UMBs. Again, because the LOADHI.COM program is not an internal MS-DOS command, its full path must be specified.

When you add device drivers or memory-resident programs in the future, you'll need to run the Optimize program again. Or, if you prefer, you can perform these operations manually with the instructions provided in the QEMM-386 manual.

Notice that the Optimize program adds the QEMM subdirectory to your computer's search path. You can remove that subdirectory from your computer's search path if you like. Consider, however, creating batch files to run QEMM-386's support programs (QEMM.COM and MFT.EXE).

You can make additional manual modifications to free more conventional memory in your computer with QEMM-386. Please see the section later in this chapter titled "Basic Memory Strategy" for more information.

Note: QEMM-386 has the ability to increase the number of UMBs available. To do this, you run the Optimize program with the /Stealth switch. Optimize will run a compatibility test for your system, which requires a floppy disk for drive A. If your system passes the test, more upper memory will be available for loading device drivers and memory-resident programs high.

QRAM

The QRAM installation program copies QRAM's files to your hard disk and incorporates QRAM commands into your CONFIG.SYS and AUTOEXEC.BAT files. Your immediate next step should be to run the Optimize program to continue the configuration of your computer. At the Command prompt, type *optimize,* and then follow the directions that appear. Your computer will reboot several times before you've finished.

The Optimize program evaluates the device drivers and memory-resident programs in your computer and then uses QRAM's Loadhi commands to load device drivers and memory-resident programs into UMBs. Although the result isn't as memory efficient as the solution provided by 386MAX or QEMM-386, it's effective on 80286-based and 8088/8086-based computers that use MS-DOS.

Note: If QRAM reports back nothing to do, either you don't have LIM EMS 4.0 memory in your computer or the EMS card is not configured properly. Consult your EMS hardware manual for instructions on how to install and configure your EMS card.

The following is a sample CONFIG.SYS file on an 80286-based PC with an Intel AboveBoard supplying LIM 4.0 expanded memory. The EMM.SYS device driver controls the expanded memory on the AboveBoard. New lines and changes are noted in *italics*.

```
device=c:\dos\himem.sys
device=c:\intel\emm.sys at 258
device=c:\qram\qram.sys r:1
dos=high
files=30
buffers=15
shell=c:\dos\command.com c:\dos\ /p
stacks=0,0
device=c:\qram\loadhi.sys /r:1 c:\mouse\mouse.sys /c1
```

The first command loads the HIMEM.SYS device driver. (HIMEM.SYS should be used instead of the QEXT.SYS extended memory manager that comes with QRAM—HIMEM.SYS is more compatible with MS-DOS.) Next comes the EMM device driver that manages expanded memory. (QRAM uses expanded memory to create UMBs.) QRAM.SYS is installed after the EMM device driver. Finally, the LOADHI.SYS device driver loads the mouse device driver into a UMB.

Note: You cannot use HIMEM.SYS on an 8088/8086-based computer, nor can you load part of MS-DOS into the HMA with the dos=high *command. Because the 8088/8086 can address only 1 MB of memory, 8088/8086-based computers can't access extended memory and therefore can't access the HMA.*

A sample AUTOEXEC.BAT file modified by QRAM is shown at the top of the next page.

```
@echo off
prompt $p$g
path c:\qram;c:\dos;c:\util;c:\mouse
set temp=c:\temp
c:\qram\loadhi /r:1 doskey /insert
```

QRAM loads memory-resident programs into UMBs with the
LOADHI.COM program. In this example, Loadhi is used to load Doskey
into a UMB. Also notice that Optimize added the QRAM subdirectory to
your computer's search path. You can remove that subdirectory from the
search path and instead run QRAM's support programs directly or, preferably, by means of batch files stored in a batch file subdirectory.

You can manually insert LOADHI.SYS and LOADHI.COM commands
when you add new device drivers or memory-resident programs to your
computer. You can also run the Optimize program again and let it reconfigure your computer for you.

BASIC MEMORY STRATEGY

When using a third-party memory manager with MS-DOS, you must reach
a compromise: Let MS-DOS do only so much, and then let the third-party
memory manager do the rest. Deciding where to let the third-party
memory manager take over can be aggravating, especially when you consider all the possibilities.

In the sections that follow, find the system most similar to yours, and then
use the information to develop an appropriate memory strategy.

'386-Based Computers Requiring Expanded Memory

The standard MS-DOS CONFIG.SYS file for '386-based computers that require expanded memory starts with these commands:

```
device=c:\dos\himem.sys
dos=high
dos=umb
device=c:\dos\emm386.exe 512 ram
```

- 386MAX, Memory Commander, and QEMM-386 come with XMS
  and EMS memory managers, eliminating the first and last
  commands.

■ Because both 386MAX and QEMM-386 also create UMBs, the Dos command no longer requires the umb option. Although Memory Commander does not admit to creating UMBs, it does basically the same thing. This means the third line can also be eliminated.

With such changes, CONFIG.SYS now looks like this:

```
Device=c:\386max\386max.sys pro=c:\386max\386max.pro
dos=high
```

Or this:

```
dos = high
device = C:\MC\MC.SYS
```

Or even this:

```
device=c:\qemm\qemm.sys RAM options
dos-high
```

The HIMEM.SYS device driver is no longer needed in these configurations. And because the EMM386.EXE expanded memory emulator becomes redundant, you can simply delete the command that loads EMM386.EXE.

386MAX, Memory Commander, and QEMM-386 simulate both extended and expanded memory. The output of the Mem command reflects this, showing large amounts of both types of memory as available and free. All three memory managers use techniques to dole out whatever type of memory is required by your applications; there's no extra work involved on your behalf.

You should continue to load your device drivers and memory-resident programs into UMBs using the Maximize or Optimize programs. With Memory Commander, you'll need to run the MC program and occasionally the MCA utility to move new device drivers and memory-resident programs into UMBs.

Note: For information on additional advantages offered by QEMM-386 and QRAM, refer to the section titled "Loading Resources into UMBs," later in this chapter.

'386-Based Computers with Windows

Windows will run in 386 enhanced mode with any of the '386 memory managers installed, as described in this chapter. As long as you specify the various Windows options during installation and read any supplemental information regarding Windows, you should experience no problems—despite the fact that these programs simulate expanded memory with extended memory.

If you do encounter a problem starting Windows, use the /3 switch as follows:

```
win /3
```

That should get Windows up and running in enhanced mode. (To verify the Windows mode, open the Help menu in the Program Manager, and select the last item, About Program Manager.)

80286-Based Computers

On most 80286-based computers, the memory strategy is twofold. The computer usually comes with extended memory. But to use UMBs and to use MS-DOS applications that don't recognize extended memory, you need expanded memory.

On 80286-based computers, this means you add an EMS 4.0 memory card to your computer. Then you install an expanded memory manager device driver. Finally you install a memory manager device driver that creates the UMBs—either MOVE'EM.MGR or QRAM.SYS.

Follow these steps, and your CONFIG.SYS file should look similar to this:

```
device=c:\dos\himem.sys
device=c:\emm.sys options
device=c:\move'em\move'em.mgr options
dos=high
```

Or this:

```
device=c:\dos\himem.sys
device=c:\emm.sys options
device=c:\qram\qram.sys options
dos=high
```

Notice that the subdirectories in the examples above are all assumed; you should specify the proper paths for all device drivers.

Finally you use your memory manager's programs to load device drivers and memory-resident programs into UMBs. If you're using QRAM with the Dos command's umb option, you can use the Devicehigh and Loadhigh commands to load device drivers and memory-resident programs into UMBs.

If you plan to run Windows, you should configure most of the memory on the memory expansion card as extended memory. (But be sure to leave enough expanded memory for applications that need it.)

8088/8086-Based Computers

The solutions for 8088/8086-based computers are, unfortunately, no better now than they were under earlier versions of MS-DOS. Your only option is to add a LIM EMS 4.0 memory expansion card to your computer and then backfill as much conventional memory as possible with expanded memory.

Both MOVE'EM and QRAM will load device drivers and memory-resident programs into UMBs if your 8088/8086-based computer has expanded memory. It's a simple solution, but it's better than no solution at all.

USING VIDEO MEMORY

Take another look at the typical computer's memory map. Refer to Figure 9-1 on the next page. Above the 640 KB is what? More memory? True. But it's video memory, used by the EGA and VGA adapters for their high-resolution graphics. You can't run programs there. Or can you?

MDA (monochrome) video systems use only 4 KB of RAM (in 80-column mode), starting at address 720,896 (memory segment B000 hex). CGA systems use only 32 KB of RAM, starting at address 753,664 (memory segment B800 hex). But both EGA and VGA use 128 KB of RAM, starting at address 655,360 (memory segment A000 hex).

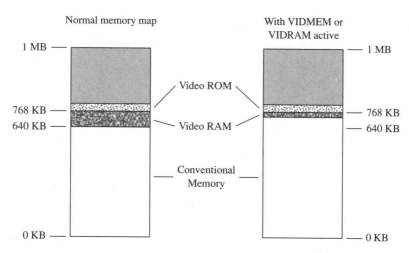

Figure 9-1. *How VIDMEM and VIDRAM can "steal" video memory.*

Memory Commander "steals" video memory for use as conventional memory. That's how you get the trademark 904 KB of conventional memory. 386MAX, QEMM-386, and QRAM also include programs that can "steal" VGA or EGA display memory and use the stolen video memory as conventional memory on computers that already have 640 KB of conventional memory. As long as you're willing to run your computer as if it had a CGA card instead of a VGA or an EGA card, you can increase MS-DOS's conventional memory by up to 96 KB.

The only drawback to this scenario is that graphics become taboo on your computer. Windows? Forget it! Don't even try running programs that use graphics—your computer might lock up. But if you don't mind sacrificing your expensive graphics, here are the individual commands that steal EGA or VGA video memory for use as conventional memory.

Note: "Stealing" video memory does not work with some combinations of computers and video cards, and can even cause your computer to lock up. Be sure you have a boot disk handy and back up your CONFIG.SYS and AUTOEXEC.BAT files before trying any of the techniques mentioned in this section. If a technique causes your computer to lock up, reboot with the boot disk and restore your old CONFIG.SYS and AUTOEXEC.BAT files.

386MAX

For 386MAX, the video memory is "stolen" by specifying the *cga* option with the command that loads 386MAX. This forces your computer into believing it has a CGA card instead of an EGA or a VGA. Voila—you get that extra 96 KB of conventional memory and can move on to the bonus round. For example:

```
device=c:\386max\386max.sys pro=c:\386max\386max.pro cga
```

Here the assumption is that you have a VGA or an EGA card and want an extra 96 KB of conventional memory. The cga option gives you that extra memory. Also, if you want to simulate an MDA card, you can use the mono option, but that gives you only an extra 64 KB of conventional memory.

You could make such a change more effectively by editing 386MAX's profile file: 386MAX keeps its options in the file 386MAX.PRO. Use the Max program to edit that file and insert the word *cga* (or *mono*) as the last line in the file. Save the file, and then reboot your computer to steal all that video memory.

Note: Run the Maximize program again when you've finished making this modification.

QEMM-386 and QRAM

QEMM-386 and QRAM owners can use the memory-resident VIDRAM program to convert VGA and EGA video memory to conventional memory. Type *vidram on* at the MS-DOS prompt to turn on video memory. Type *vidram off* at the MS-DOS prompt to turn off video memory, which allows you to run your graphics programs again (but shrinks MS-DOS back to below 640 KB).

If you use QEMM-386, you should first add the *vidramega* option to the end of the Device command that loads QEMM386.SYS in CONFIG.SYS. Then add the following two lines to the end of your AUTOEXEC.BAT file:

```
c:\qemm\loadhi c:\qemm\vidram.com resident
c:\qemm\vidram on
```

The first command loads the Vidram program into a UMB and makes it resident. The second command turns on video memory, giving you up to

96 KB additional conventional memory. Wow. (Run the optimize program after making these changes.)

The Vidram command works in nearly the same way for QRAM users, but QRAM lacks the vidramega option. Plus, QRAM users should specify *on* instead of *resident* when loading Vidram into a UMB. To do this, add these two lines to the end of your AUTOEXEC.BAT file:

```
c:\qemm\loadhi c:\qemm\vidram.com on
c:\qemm\vidram on
```

The neat thing about the Vidram command is that you can use it to turn off video memory and get back your graphics memory. So if you suddenly decide that you want to use your VGA in the 50-row mode or run a graphics application, you can type *vidram off.*

Note: *If you forget and try to run a graphics application, Vidram will remind you that graphics modes are disabled and present the option of quitting the application.*

LOADING RESOURCES INTO UMBs

Third-party memory managers have one advantage over MS-DOS: They can "steal" video memory. But that's not always compatible with Windows and other graphics applications.

Another advantage offered by the Quarterdeck products is the ability to load system resources into UMBs. Regardless of your graphics needs, the result is more conventional memory for your computer.

What are system resources anyway? Well, they're those files, buffers, and storage places that MS-DOS needs in order to operate. Unfortunately, they also occupy conventional memory. Here's a list of common system resources and the amount of memory each uses.

Resource	Conventional memory used
Buffers	532 bytes per buffer
FCBs	None (needed only for compatibility; use the Files command instead)
Files	About 53 bytes for each file
Lastdrive	About 80 bytes for each drive letter after E

It might seem silly to load these resources into UMBs when the space to be gained appears minimal. But when your computer is low on memory, every byte counts. The following sections describe each of these system resources in greater detail.

Buffers

The Buffers command sets aside space for MS-DOS to use when reading and writing files to disk. In a way, the buffers are like a mini-disk cache, storing information so that MS-DOS can read from and write to disk more efficiently. This is why more buffers are required by disk-intensive programs (and why fewer buffers are required when you're running a disk cache like SMARTDrive).

The downside is, regardless of how many buffers you have, they take up memory. QEMM-386 and QRAM come with the BUFFERS.COM program, which allocates upper memory for MS-DOS's buffers instead of allocating memory elsewhere.

To use BUFFERS.COM, follow these steps:

1. Edit the Buffers command in the CONFIG.SYS file to equal only one buffer:

   ```
   buffers=1
   ```

2. Add the following command on the second line of your AUTOEXEC.BAT file:

   ```
   c:\qemm\loadhi c:\qemm\buffers=15
   ```

This command brings the total number of buffers available to MS-DOS up to 15. If you need more buffers, specify a larger value. Be sure to specify the correct path for QEMM-386's (or QRAM's) Loadhi and Buffers program. In this example, the C:\QEMM subdirectory is assumed.

It's important to insert the Buffers command at the top of your AUTOEXEC.BAT file, immediately after *@echo off*. Placing the Buffers command near the top of AUTOEXEC.BAT lets other commands take advantage of the disk buffering.

FCBs

File Control Blocks, or FCBs, were used by programs that operated under MS-DOS version 1. Although MS-DOS version 2.0 introduced a more efficient method of file handling, the Fcbs command was retained for compatibility with older software. If you have a program that absolutely requires FCBs, use the Fcbs command. Otherwise, use the Files command.

QEMM-386 and QRAM have an FCBS.COM program, which can be used to load FCBs into a UMB. If, and only if, you have a program that refuses to run without the Fcbs command, use QEMM-386's or QRAM's FCBS.COM program with the Loadhi command to load the FCBs into a UMB. This technique is similar to the Files command, and it's fully illustrated in the QEMM-386 and QRAM manuals.

Files

The MS-DOS Files command sets the number of files that MS-DOS can have open at one time. MS-DOS keeps track of open files by using a small amount of memory (about 53 bytes) called a *file handle*. MS-DOS needs one file handle for each open file. Some database and accounting packages require that you set the number of files that MS-DOS can have open to 32 or more. That's not a large amount of memory (about 1.6 KB), but every byte adds up.

The memory for file handles is allocated when your computer boots. MS-DOS typically uses conventional memory for the file handles. QEMM-386 and QRAM come with a program called FILES.COM that can use memory from a UMB for the file handles. To use FILES.COM, follow these steps:

1. Place the following command in your CONFIG.SYS file:

```
files=10
```

2. Place the following command in your AUTOEXEC.BAT file:

```
c:\qemm\loadhi c:\qemm\files=32
```

These commands let MS-DOS have up to 32 files open simultaneously. The memory for 22 file handles comes from a UMB, and the memory for the other 10 file handles comes from conventional memory. Be sure to specify the correct path for QEMM-386's (or QRAM's) Loadhi and Files programs. In this example, the C:\QEMM subdirectory is assumed.

Lastdrive

The Lastdrive command allows you to set the highest available drive letter in your computer. By default, MS-DOS allows drive letters up to the letter E. Beyond that, you use the Lastdrive command to reserve more drive letters, all the way up through the letter Z. But you pay a price of about 80 bytes per drive letter beyond E.

Note: The Lastdrive command is also used for network drives and for those who use the Subst command to assign drive letters to subdirectories (which can be handy).

QEMM-386 and QRAM come with a program called LASTDRIV.COM, which allocates memory for additional drive letters from a UMB. You can use this program even if you have drives up through only the letter C.

To use LASTDRIV.COM, follow these steps:

1. Edit or insert the Lastdrive command in your CONFIG.SYS file. Set Lastdrive to the highest drive letter in your computer (and don't forget any RAM disks). For example,

```
lastdrive=d
```

2. Add the following command near the top of AUTOEXEC.BAT:

```
c:\qemm\loadhi c:\qemm\lastdriv z
```

This command reserves drive letters up through Z without losing any conventional memory but still giving you the option to add those drives in the future. Be sure to use the proper path for Loadhi and Lastdrive. In this example, the C:\QEMM subdirectory is assumed.

THE FINAL RESULTS

Using optimal configuration commands, the following are the final versions of the sample CONFIG.SYS and AUTOEXEC.BAT files presented early in this chapter. (Note that these are optimal configurations for my computer; yours might differ.) Further examples of other configurations are covered in Chapter 10.

Following each of the configurations is the amount of available memory remaining when my computer runs the configuration (as shown by the

Mem command). Remember, your CONFIG.SYS and AUTOEXEC.BAT files will be different, depending on your requirements. The files shown here are samples only (although they all work and produce the available memory indicated).

Note: For compatibility, the video memory stealing options were removed from the final configuration of 386 MAX and QEMM-386.

386MAX

CONFIG.SYS:

```
Device=c:\386max\386max.sys pro=c:\386max\386max.pro
dos=high
files=30
buffers=15
shell=c:\dos\command.com c:\dos\ /p
stacks=0,0
device=C:\386MAX\386load.sys size=11504 prgreg=3 prog=c:\dos\setver.exe
device=C:\386MAX\386load.sys size=5888 prgreg=3
 prog=c:\dos\ramdrive.sys 512 /e
device=C:\386MAX\386load.sys size=9072 prgreg=3 prog=c:\dos\ansi.sys
```

AUTOEXEC.BAT:

```
@echo off
prompt $p$g
path c:\dos;c:\util;c:\mouse
set temp=c:\temp
C:\386MAX\386load size=41824 flexframe prog=smartdrv
C:\386MAX\386load size=56928 flexframe prog=mouse
C:\386MAX\386load size=6400 prgreg=3 flexframe prog=doskey /insert
```

MEM:

```
Memory Type        Total =  Used  +  Free
----------------   ------   ------    ------
Conventional        640K     16K      624K
Upper                 0K      0K        0K
Adapter RAM/ROM     384K     384K       0K
Extended (XMS)     3072K    1968K     1104K
----------------   ------   ------    ------
Total memory       4096K    2368K     1728K

Total under 1 MB    640K     16K      624K

Total Expanded (EMS)                  1680K  (1720320 bytes)
Total Expanded (EMS)                  1104K  (1130496 bytes)
Largest executable program size        623K   (638416 bytes)
Largest free upper memory block          0K       (0 bytes)
MS-DOS is resident in the high memory area.
```

Memory Commander

CONFIG.SYS:

```
break = off
buffers = 15
files = 30
stacks = 0,0
dos = high
device = C:\MC\MC.SYS
rem device=c:\dos\himem.sys
shell=c:\dos\command.com c:\dos\ /p
device=c:\dos\setver.exe
device=c:\dos\ramdrive.sys 512 /e
rem device=c:\dos\ansi.sys
```

AUTOEXEC.BAT:

```
@echo off
prompt $p$g
path c:\dos;c:\util;c:\mouse
set temp=c:\temp
smartdrv
mouse
doskey /insert

c:\mc\mca.exe auto optimize
```

MEM:

```
Memory Type       Total =  Used  +  Free
----------------  ------   ------   ------
Conventional       760K     18K     742K
Upper                0K      0K       0K
Adapter RAM/ROM    264K     264K      0K
Extended (XMS)    3072K    2128K     944K
----------------  ------   ------   ------
Total memory      4096K    2410K    1686K

Total under 1 MB   760K     18K     742K

Total Expanded (EMS)                  2480K  (2539520 bytes)
Free Expanded (EMS)                    944K  (966656 bytes)
Largest executable program size        742K  (759968 bytes)
Largest free upper memory block          0K       (0 bytes)
MS-DOS is resident in the high memory area.
```

QEMM-386

CONFIG.SYS:

```
DEVICE=C:\QEMM\QEMM386.SYS RAM
dos=high
files=10
buffers=1
lastdrive=d
shell=c:\dos\command.com c:\dos\ /p
stacks=0,0
device=c:\qemm\loadhi.sys /r:1 c:\dos\setver.exe
device=c:\qemm\loadhi.sys /r:3 c:\dos\ramdrive.sys 512 /e
device=c:\qemm\loadhi.sys /r:1 c:\dos\ansi.sys
```

AUTOEXEC.BAT:

```
@echo off
c:\qemm\loadhi c:\qemm\buffers=15
c:\qemm\loadhi c:\qemm\files=32
c:\qemm\loadhi c:\qemm\lastdriv z
prompt $p$g
path c:\qemm;c:\dos;c:\util;c:\mouse
set temp=c:\temp
c:\qemm\loadhi /r:2 smartdrv
c:\qemm\loadhi /r:2 mouse
c:\qemm\loadhi /r:1 doskey /insert
```

MEM:

```
Memory Type        Total =  Used  +  Free
----------------   ------   ------   ------
Conventional        640K     26K     614K
Upper                 0K      0K       0K
Adapter RAM/ROM     384K     384K      0K
Extended (XMS)     3072K    1888K    1184K
----------------   ------   ------   ------
Total memory       4096K    2298K    1798K

Total under 1 MB    640K     26K     614K

Total Expanded (EMS)               3360K  (3440640 bytes)
Free Expanded (EMS)                1184K  (1212416 bytes)
Largest executable program size     621K  (636000 bytes)
Largest free upper memory block       0K       (0 bytes)
MS-DOS is resident in the high memory area.
```

Conclusion

You might be able to achieve better results than this. To find out, grab your memory manager and *read its manual*. You know the terms. You know what's where in memory. Now it will be easier to understand what the memory managers do and how you can take advantage of them.

SUMMARY

Memory management beyond what MS-DOS offers is possible and beneficial. On '386-based computers, third-party memory-management products can make kilobytes of extra conventional memory available for your applications, MS-DOS, and Microsoft Windows.

- 386MAX, Memory Commander, and QEMM-386 are all memory-management products for '386-based computers. They supplement the memory power MS-DOS gives you, managing extended and expanded memory and performing other memory services.

- 386MAX's MOVE'EM and QRAM are memory-management products for 80286-based and 8088/8086-based computers. They give 80286-based computers the ability to load device drivers and memory-resident programs into UMBs.

- Installation and optimization of the 386MAX, QEMM-386, and QRAM memory managers is greatly facilitated by the Maximize and Optimize programs. The Maximize and Optimize programs will fine-tune your computer's configuration for optimal memory performance.

- Memory Commander maintains its optimization information in a special database file. That file, updated and maintained with the MCA utility, tells Memory Commander what to do with your device drivers and memory-resident programs. The benefit here is that your CONFIG.SYS and AUTOEXEC.BAT files don't become littered with complex memory-management commands.

- Each of the memory managers covered in this chapter is compatible with Windows (although they might require some tweaking).

- QEMM-386 and QRAM have the ability to load your computer resources into UMBs, freeing even more conventional memory.

- On computers with 640 KB of conventional memory and EGA or VGA video adaptors, you can get up to 96 KB more conventional memory by using the VIDRAM.COM program that comes with QEMM-386 and QRAM, or the cga option with 386MAX. In some configurations, that's up to 736 KB free conventional memory.

- Memory Commander stakes its reputation on stealing video memory. In some configurations, it's possible to have up to 904 KB free conventional memory. On my test machines, a more realistic value was 736 KB free—which is still a huge chunk of RAM.

- In the end, what you get out of your computer depends on what you have in it. These memory managers will help in varying degrees, each of them offering that much more than what MS-DOS gives you. For a modest investment, you can get more free memory out of the same computer—without plugging in RAM chips.

Chapter 10

Setup Scenarios

The 386MAX manual mentions that, given only conventional and upper memory plus five device drivers and memory-resident programs, you can have up to 3840 possible loading configurations. Multiply that by some 60 million computers, and you can see why a book that promised the definitive CONFIG.SYS and AUTOEXEC.BAT files for everyone would make the Los Angeles County phone book look like a pamphlet. Accordingly, this chapter focuses on several typical setup scenarios for a variety of situations and provides general and specific memory solutions for each. By using the setup that most closely resembles your own situation, and by taking advantage of the information in the other chapters in this book, your experiences with running out of memory will be, well...just a memory.

GENERAL SUGGESTIONS

Whatever your situation might be, you can take three steps that are guaranteed to help your computer get the most from memory:

- Add more memory whenever possible.

- Explore the MS-DOS solutions, and consider a third-party memory manager.

- Install a RAM disk and/or a disk cache.

The following sections describe these steps in more detail.

8088/8086-Based Computers

MS-DOS memory solutions for 8088/8086-based computers are rare. Third-party memory managers are your best bet for solving memory problems. Follow these steps.

1. **Add a LIM EMS 4.0 memory card to your computer.** Disable all but 256 KB of your conventional memory, and backfill the remaining 384 KB with expanded memory for a total of 640 KB of conventional memory.

2. **Pack the EMS card with as much memory as possible.** Buy at least 1 MB of memory. (If you find inexpensive memory, buy 2 MB.) A good strategy is to fill your EMS card to its maximum RAM potential. This prevents your having to open the computer's case again to add memory.

3. **Install your EMM device driver.** The EMM (expanded memory manager) device driver comes with your LIM EMS 4.0 memory card. You add the command that loads the EMM device driver in your CONFIG.SYS file.

4. **Install a third-party memory manager.** Although Chapter 9 contains memory solutions for 8088/8086-based computers, remember: The 8088/8086 peaked long ago, and memory solutions for this system will soon disappear. When you upgrade, buy a '386-compatible computer.

5. **Take advantage of memory.** Some applications can directly use your expanded memory. If your applications don't use expanded memory, consider creating a RAM disk and/or a disk cache. Refer to Chapter 7 for more information.

80286-Based Computers

Although no amount of software will give an 80286-based computer the memory-management capabilities of a '386, you can enhance memory management through the following steps:

1. **Add extended memory to your computer.** Most 80286-based computers come with 1 MB of RAM: 640 KB of conventional memory and 384 KB of extended memory. Some programs (such as Microsoft Windows) and utilities (such as RAM disks and disk caches) will use extended memory. For RAM disks and disk caches, extended memory is great! If you want a larger RAM disk, buy extended memory for your 80286-based computer. But this is only half the solution.

2. **Add a LIM EMS 4.0 memory card to your computer.** And backfill as much conventional memory as possible.

3. **Pack the EMS card with as much memory as possible.** Most EMS cards come with 512 KB of RAM. However, I suggest you pack the card full of RAM immediately. This prevents your having to open the computer's case again to add memory.

4. **Install your memory-management device drivers.** Under MS-DOS, you will need three memory-management device drivers: HIMEM.SYS, the EMM device driver that came with your EMS card, and the third-party memory-management device driver. The coordination of these three memory managers is covered in Chapter 9.

5. **Use the memory capabilities of MS-DOS.** For an 80286-based computer, load part of MS-DOS into the HMA using the Dos command.

6. **Load device drivers and memory-resident programs into UMBs.** With the third-party memory manager, you can load your device drivers and memory-resident programs into UMBs. If the memory manager allows it, you can also load system resources into UMBs or "steal" video memory to add to conventional memory.

7. **Take advantage of the new memory.** Some applications will take immediate advantage of your expanded memory, whereas others might need your extended memory. If no applications use expanded or extended memory, create a RAM disk and a disk cache to improve your computer's performance.

'386-Based Computers

MS-DOS and third-party memory managers offer the most benefits to '386-based computers. Follow these steps:

1. **Add extended memory to your computer.** Be sure all the memory you add is installed on the motherboard or in a special 32-bit memory card slot. Add as much memory as you can afford. (And remember to add it in the increments that are appropriate for your computer or memory board.)

2. **Use the MS-DOS memory-management commands.** First install the HIMEM.SYS extended memory device driver, and then use the Dos command twice to load part of MS-DOS into the HMA and prepare MS-DOS for the UMBs. Finally, install the EMM386.EXE device driver to create the UMBs, simulate expanded memory, or both. Or you can use third-party memory managers to take the place of both HIMEM.SYS and EMM386.EXE. The Dos command is still required to load part of MS-DOS into the HMA.

3. **Load device drivers and memory-resident programs into UMBs.** If your third-party memory manager supports it, also load your system resources into UMBs. (Refer to Chapter 9.)

4. **Choose your computer's configuration.** Use EMM386.EXE to simulate expanded memory with extended memory if any of your applications require expanded memory. Sometimes a compromise must be reached: For example, maintain 2 MB of extended memory for a RAM disk, and use the rest to simulate expanded memory. Make your decision, and configure your computer accordingly.

5. **Steal video memory.** If you're not going to be using graphics, consider using extra EGA or VGA video memory to extend the MS-DOS conventional memory limit. 386MAX, Memory Commander, and QEMM-386 all let you do this. (Refer to the section "Using Video Memory" in Chapter 9.)

6. **Take advantage of memory.** Start working with applications that use extended or expanded memory. If you have memory left over, consider creating a RAM disk or a disk cache. (The benefits of each are covered in Chapter 7.)

SCENARIOS

On the following pages, you'll find descriptions of sample computers: their hardware and software configurations, as well as complementary CONFIG.SYS and AUTOEXEC.BAT files that serve as possible solutions to memory problems. From these examples, you can apply the solutions to your own situation and computer.

'386 Windows Computer

Description: A Dell 486D with an i486 microprocessor and 2 MB of RAM. Windows requires at least 2 MB total memory in a '386-based computer to run in enhanced mode. But the more memory you add, the faster Windows runs.

Strategy: Add 2 MB of memory to your computer, bringing the total amount of RAM to 4 MB. Better still, add 6 MB of RAM to bring everything up to 8 MB. (Actually, you should add as much memory as you can afford.)

Steps: Add two 1-MB SIMMs to the computer's motherboard.

Note: After upgrading this computer, or after you add extended memory to any 80286-based or '386-based computer, you'll see a memory error message when your computer boots. To fix the error, simply run your computer's setup program to tell your computer about the new memory.

To run Windows on this computer, you'll want to configure all memory as extended memory. But to have as much free conventional memory as possible, you'll want to load device drivers and memory-resident programs into UMBs.

This computer's CONFIG.SYS starts with the following lines:

```
device=c:\windows\himem.sys
dos=high
dos=umb
device=c:\dos\emm386.exe noems
```

HIMEM.SYS is an extended memory manager. The Dos commands load part of MS-DOS into the HMA and prepare MS-DOS for the UMBs. Then the EMM386.EXE expanded memory emulator creates those UMBs but doesn't use any extended memory to simulate expanded memory.

At this point, you use the Devicehigh command to load your device drivers—such as RAMDRIVE.SYS—into UMBs. Then use Loadhigh in AUTOEXEC.BAT to load any memory-resident programs. Keep in mind that this is a Windows-based machine and probably won't need MS-DOS device drivers and memory-resident programs (such as ANSI.SYS, Doskey, and so on). (Refer to Chapter 8.)

'386 Windows Computer
Requiring Expanded Memory

Description: A Gateway 2000, 486/33 machine with 8 MB of memory. This is plenty of memory for Windows, however this system also runs MS-DOS applications that require expanded memory.

Strategy: Set up EMM386.EXE to provide both extended and expanded memory. Do this by specifying the ram option instead of the noems option.

Steps: Edit CONFIG.SYS accordingly.

Normally Windows runs with EMM386.EXE's noems option. The noems option directs EMM386.EXE to provide UMBs but not expanded memory. The RAM option also provides UMBs, but directs EMM386.EXE to supply expanded memory. If a specific value isn't specified, expanded memory will be supplied on an as-needed basis. This is the most effective way to solve the expanded-memory-under-Windows dilemma.

This computer's CONFIG.SYS begins with the following lines:

```
device=c:\dos\himem.sys
dos=high
dos=umb
device=c:\dos\emm386.exe ram
```

HIMEM.SYS provides the extended memory management. The Dos commands load part of MS-DOS into the HMA and prepare MS-DOS for the UMBs. Then the EMM386.EXE expanded memory emulator creates UMBs and provides expanded memory as necessary. The Mem command's output proves this:

```
Memory Type       Total = Used  +  Free
----------------  ------   ------   ------
Conventional       640K     74K      566K
Upper               91K     34K       57K
Adapter RAM/ROM    293K    293K        0K
Extended (XMS)*   7168K   2880K     4288K
----------------  ------   ------   ------
Total memory      8192K   3281K     4911K
```

```
Total under 1 MB     731K      65K      666K

Total Expanded (EMS)                7744K (7929856 bytes)
Free Expanded (EMS)*                7072K (7241728 bytes)

* EMM386 is using XMS memory to simulate EMS memory as needed.
  Free EMS memory may change as free XMS memory changes.

Largest executable program size     575K  (588416 bytes)
Largest free upper memory block      57K   (58192 bytes)
MS-DOS is resident in the high memory area.
```

Above, nearly equal amounts of extended and expanded memory are available. In Windows, the expanded memory will be available to any MS-DOS application, providing that program's PIF file specifies expanded memory. (The "default" PIF file automatically provides 1024 KB of expanded memory to all MS-DOS applications run under Windows.)

'386 MS-DOS Computer

Description: A COMPAQ DESKPRO with an 80386 microprocessor and 2 MB of RAM. This is a typical amount of memory for a PC, although most '386 machines should have at least 4 MB of RAM installed (especially if you want to run Windows). This computer will run text-only MS-DOS applications, but not graphics applications or Microsoft Windows.

Strategy: Add 2 MB of RAM to your computer, bringing the total up to 4 MB. Even if none of your applications require this much memory, the balance can be used to supplement hard disk performance as a RAM disk or disk cache.

Steps: Add two 1-MB memory modules to the DESKPRO's memory card. These memory modules are not DIPs, SIPs, or SIMMs, but actual cards that plug into the DESKPRO's memory card. It's safest to purchase these memory modules directly from COMPAQ rather than from a third party.

How you configure the 4 MB is up to you. The following snippet from CONFIG.SYS (at the top of the next page) shows how QEMM would configure this system, splitting up extended memory 50/50: 2048 KB of extended memory and 2048 KB of expanded memory.

```
device=c:\qemm\qemm386.sys ram vidramega extmem=2048
dos=high
buffers=15
files=10
lastdrive=d
device=c:\qemm\loadhi.sys c:\dos\ramdrive.sys 1024 /e
```

In this example, QEMM386.SYS is installed first using the Device command; HIMEM.SYS and EMM386.EXE are not needed. QEMM386.SYS is followed by several options: ram, which creates the UMBs; vidramega, which "steals" 96 KB of VGA video memory for conventional memory; and extmem=2048, which leaves 2 MB of extended memory for use as a RAM disk or a disk cache (both of which work better in extended memory).

Part of MS-DOS is loaded into the HMA with the Dos command above, and it seems as though the Files and Lastdrive commands are a little low—but they're actually loaded into UMBs by special QEMM-386 programs in the AUTOEXEC.BAT file. (Refer to Chapter 9.)

Finally QEMM-386's LOADHI.SYS program loads the RAMDRIVE.SYS device driver into a UMB. Notice that the 1-MB RAM disk is created in extended memory—the extended memory that was left by QEMM.SYS at the start of the CONFIG.SYS file. (It's assumed that SMARTDrive in AUTOEXEC.BAT will use the remainder of extended memory.)

'386 General-Purpose Computer

Description: A typical 80386SX laptop with 2 MB of RAM and VGA graphics.

Strategy: Upgrade the computer to its full memory potential. (Suppose, for this example, that it's 8 MB of RAM.)

Steps: Install six 1-MB SIMMs on the motherboard.

This computer needs to be flexible: At times it's an MS-DOS computer that has expanded memory. But because this computer also runs graphics applications and—occasionally—Windows, it's best to select 386MAX, which sets up CONFIG.SYS as follows:

```
device=c:\386max\386max.sys pro=c:\386max\386max.pro
dos=high
```

In this example, the Device command loads the 386MAX.SYS device driver into memory. The file 386MAX.PRO contains 386MAX options. (During 386MAX's installation, it was indicated that the computer might run Windows; therefore, all 386MAX options have been set properly for Windows.)

The Dos command loads part of MS-DOS into the HMA. From there, 386MAX's special commands will be used to load device drivers and memory-resident programs into UMBs.

Notice that the vidmem option for 386MAX is not specified on this computer. Although it would give an extra 96 KB to conventional memory, it would be incompatible with graphics applications and Windows.

80286 Windows Computer

Description: An original IBM AT computer with an 80286 microprocessor and 512 KB of RAM.

Strategy: Purchase an Intel Above Board. The Above Board can supply the computer with both extended and expanded memory. To use Windows, your computer needs at least 256 KB of extended memory, but you'd like to backfill conventional memory with expanded memory to take advantage of LIM EMS 4.0-compatible applications.

Steps: Pack the Above Board with as much memory as it can hold (2 MB). Configure 1 MB as extended memory and the other megabyte as expanded memory. The expanded memory will be used to backfill conventional memory and to create the UMBs, and the extended memory will be used by Windows.

Three device drivers are needed to manage all this memory: An extended memory manager, an expanded memory manager, and a memory manager to create the UMBs from expanded memory. QRAM makes a good choice for this computer. The CONFIG.SYS file for this computer is shown at the top of the next page.

```
device=c:\windows\himem.sys
device=c:\intel\emm.sys at 1024
device=c:\qram\qram.sys r:1
dos=high
buffers=10
files=10
lastdrive=c
```

HIMEM.SYS is the extended memory manager that also allows MS-DOS to access the HMA. EMM.SYS is Intel's expanded memory manager. Then QRAM's memory manager, QRAM.SYS, maps expanded memory into the vacant areas in upper memory to create UMBs.

The Dos command loads part of MS-DOS into the HMA and prepares MS-DOS for the UMBs. QRAM.SYS creates the UMBs. QRAM's own Loadhi commands are then used to load device drivers and memory-resident programs into the UMBs.

The Files and Lastdrive commands are deliberately set to low values; counterpart QRAM commands are specified in AUTOEXEC.BAT to create file handles and space for additional drive letters in UMBs.

Spreadsheet Computer

Description: Spreadsheets require a lot of memory. For example, Lotus 1-2-3 for MS-DOS can use up to 640 KB of conventional memory and 4 MB of expanded memory. To check your memory usage, type the command /, *Worksheet, Global* while running 1-2-3. The memory usage is displayed in the top center of the screen.

If you load Lotus 1-2-3 on the typical MS-DOS computer, with part of MS-DOS loaded into the HMA and a few device drivers loaded into UMBs, you might see up to 415 KB of available conventional memory, plus the amount of expanded memory you've installed in your computer or the amount being simulated by extended memory. (Remember, Lotus 1-2-3 was the original inspiration for expanded memory.)

Strategy: The best way to add expanded memory to a '386-based computer is to add extended memory and then simulate expanded memory with extended memory, using EMM386.EXE or a third-party memory manager.

Steps: For example, suppose you have a fast i486-based computer to make Lotus 1-2-3 sizzle. This computer has 4 MB of RAM on a memory expansion card in a special 32-bit memory card slot. To simulate 4 MB of expanded memory, use the following lines in CONFIG.SYS:

```
device=c:\dos\himem.sys
dos=high
dos=umb
device=c:\dos\emm386.exe 4096 ram
```

HIMEM.SYS is installed first, and then the Dos commands are used to load part of MS-DOS into the HMA and prepare MS-DOS for the UMBs. The EMM386.EXE device driver is used to simulate 4 MB of expanded memory using extended memory, as well as to create the UMBs (thanks to the ram option).

If this computer had a VGA or EGA graphics card, you could use one of the third-party memory managers to steal some of the video memory for conventional memory. (But note that you might have to reconfigure Lotus 1-2-3 to run in CGA mode.)

Networked System

Description: A 1-MB 80286-based computer hooked up to a network—a "diskless workstation." All hard disk storage is provided by the network file server. This computer has a 1.2-MB floppy-disk drive, which is used to boot the computer. There's room for extended memory, and there are expansion slots into which you could plug a LIM EMS 4.0 memory card.

Strategy: Add expanded memory and move the network device drivers into UMBs. MS-DOS cannot do this alone on an 80286-based computer, so you need a third-party memory manager plus the LIM EMS 4.0 memory card. You must create an interesting boot disk containing the network device drivers and programs, the MS-DOS programs, and the memory managers. But by eliminating unneeded files, a 1.2-MB disk should have enough space to hold all the files necessary to boot the computer and connect it to the network.

Steps: Install an LIM EMS 4.0 memory card in your computer. The EMS card should have as much memory as possible, with a 512-KB minimum.

On the software side, install the HIMEM.SYS extended memory manager to allow MS-DOS to access the HMA. Next install your expanded memory manager and the third-party memory manager. Use the third-party memory manager's commands to load your network device drivers and memory-resident programs into UMBs. If you use QRAM, you can use MS-DOS's Devicehigh and Loadhigh commands instead (which saves on boot disk space). For example,

```
device=a:\dos\himem.sys
device=a:\emm.sys at 258
device=a:\qram\qram.sys r:1
dos=high,umb
```

The AUTOEXEC.BAT file will contain commands similar to this:

```
loadhigh a:\novell\ipx.com
loadhigh a:\novell\net5.com
```

In the future you could add extended memory and create a large RAM disk. For example, if you added 4 MB of extended memory, you could use the RAMDRIVE.SYS device driver to create a 4-MB RAM disk. Disk-intensive applications could then be transferred from the server to the RAM disk and would run very fast. After adding the extended memory, you'd place the following command in your CONFIG.SYS file (after the memory-management commands):

```
device=a:\qram\loadhi.sys r:1 a:\ramdrive.sys 4096 /e
```

QRAM's Loadhi command loads the RAM-disk device driver into a UMB; *4096* is the size of the RAM disk (4 MB); and the /e switch creates the RAM disk in extended memory.

Note: Run QRAM's Optimize program to ensure that the device drivers and memory-resident programs are loaded into the proper upper memory regions.

SUMMARY

Getting the best performance out of your computer requires adding memory to your computer, figuring out what type of memory your applications need, and then configuring the memory accordingly.

MS-DOS works best on '386-based computers. Conventional memory can be freed by loading part of MS-DOS into the HMA and loading device drivers and memory-resident programs into UMBs. Extended memory is available for those applications that require it. The extended memory can be used to simulate expanded memory if any of your applications require expanded memory.

For 80286-based and 8088/8086-based computers, the MS-DOS solutions are more limited, but third-party memory managers can give you the same power—and sometimes more—that MS-DOS provides.

The best solution for 8088/8086-based and 80286-based computers is a combination of MS-DOS and a third-party memory manager. Consider the following:

- How much memory can I afford to add to my computer?

- Can I add and use a LIM EMS 4.0 memory card in my 80286-based or 8088/8086-based computer? (If you can, use it to backfill conventional memory with expanded memory.)

- What type of memory do my applications require? Do they need extended or expanded memory, and how much of each?

- Which CONFIG.SYS commands load my extended and expanded memory managers?

- Part of MS-DOS should always be loaded into the HMA on 80286-based and '386-based computers. (This is an answer, not a question. Unfortunately, the HMA doesn't exist on 8088/8086-based PCs.)

- Device drivers and memory-resident programs should be loaded into UMBs when possible.

- If your third-party memory manager supports it, load your system resources into UMBs.

- If you have an EGA or a VGA graphics card but don't need EGA or VGA graphics, let a third-party memory manager steal some of your graphics card's video memory for conventional memory.

■ After you're satisfied with CONFIG.SYS and AUTOEXEC.BAT, *leave them alone!*

It always takes time and trouble to get everything "just right" in your CONFIG.SYS and AUTOEXEC.BAT files. This is why those installation programs that change your CONFIG.SYS and AUTOEXEC.BAT files can be so annoying. I have one final suggestion: Copy your final, pristine CONFIG.SYS and AUTOEXEC.BAT files to your MS-DOS subdirectory. Use the Attrib command to make the files read-only, as follows:

```
C:\DOS>attrib c:\dos\autoexec.bat +r
C:\DOS>attrib c:\dos\config.sys +r
```

These files will serve as backups if anything happens to the original files.

Appendix A

Glossary

'386 An Intel 80386SX, 80386, i486SX, i486, 486DX2, or similar microprocessor. Thanks to the advanced, built-in memory-mapping capabilities of these chips, MS-DOS can do wondrous things with memory—without extra hardware.

80286 An Intel 80286 or similar microprocessor. Although this chip can access up to 16 MB of memory, it lacks the memory-mapping capabilities of the '386 family.

8088/8086 An Intel 8088 or 8086, NEC V20 or V30, or similar microprocessor. MS-DOS doesn't have a real memory solution for these chips, but third-party memory managers in combination with a LIM EMS 4.0 memory expansion card will work wonders for computers that use these chips.

address A location in memory. Each location in memory has an address — a specific place somewhere in conventional memory, upper memory, or extended memory.

address space The total amount of memory a microprocessor can access. The 8088/8086 has a 1-MB address space, the 80286 has a 16-MB address space, and the '386 has a 4096-MB address space (except for the 80386SX, which has an address space of 16 MB).

backfill The process in which an EMS memory card maps expanded memory into conventional memory to bring the total amount of conventional memory up to 640 KB. A strategy worth using on 8088/8086-based and 80286-based computers to get the most from EMS 4.0 is to disable all but 256 KB of conventional memory. Let a LIM EMS 4.0 memory card map expanded memory into the disabled 384 KB. This 384-KB region acts like one big page frame; expanded memory can be mapped in and out of this region.

179

BIOS Basic Input/Output System. The BIOS is a set of routines stored in ROM chips. These routines work closely with the computer's hardware to support the transfer of information between parts of your computer, such as memory, disk drives, and the monitor. The BIOS is invisible to computer users—only programmers need to access the BIOS.

bit A binary digit, either a 1 or a 0 in the binary number system. A bit is the smallest unit of information a computer can handle.

byte A group of 8 bits used to represent a value from 0 through 255, which in turn ultimately represents a single alphanumeric character, graphics character, or special control character. Therefore, a byte can be thought of as a single character of information.

conventional memory The lower 640 KB of memory, from memory location 0 through 655,359. This is where MS-DOS and applications normally run.

device driver A control program that permits a computer to communicate with a device such as a disk drive or a mouse.

Devicehigh The MS-DOS command that loads device drivers into upper memory blocks. It's roughly equivalent to the Device command, with the addition of the size option.

DIP Dual In-line Package. The traditional RAM chip package.

disk cache A portion of memory that stores information read from disk. If the computer needs that information again, it reads the information from the disk cache rather than from disk.

DRAM Dynamic Random Access Memory. An inexpensive type of memory chip that needs periodic refreshing ("recharging"). The majority of memory chips in a computer are DRAMs.

EMM *See* expanded memory manager.

EMS *See* expanded memory specification.

expanded memory Memory that is not normally in a microprocessor's address space. Think of it as a pool of extra memory that MS-DOS can access via an EMS device driver.

expanded memory manager A device driver that implements the software portion of the expanded memory specification (EMS). Although EMS systems typically require additional hardware, EMMs written for '386 microprocessors can use the advanced memory-mapping capabilities of these chips to simulate expanded memory by using extended memory.

expanded memory specification A technique for adding memory to IBM PCs and compatible computers; also known as LIM (Lotus-Intel-Microsoft) EMS.

extended memory Memory above 1 MB on 80286-based and '386-based computers. It is accessible only when the microprocessor is in protected mode. Because MS-DOS runs in real mode, extended memory is not usually available to MS-DOS applications. *See also* extended memory specification.

extended memory specification A specification that defines a software interface to allow real-mode applications to use extended memory. The management of extended memory is provided by a device driver called an extended memory manager. MS-DOS provides the HIMEM.SYS device driver for managing extended memory.

gigabyte (GB) Roughly 1 billion bytes.

high-DOS memory Another term for upper memory.

high memory area The first 64 KB of extended memory on an 80286-based or '386-based computer. The HIMEM.SYS device driver lets MS-DOS access the high memory area (HMA). The Dos command loads part of MS-DOS into the HMA, freeing about 50 KB of conventional memory.

HMA *See* high memory area.

interleaving A method of speeding memory access by splitting memory into two logical regions. One region is refreshed while the other is accessed. This improves the computer's overall performance.

kilobyte (KB) Roughly 1000 bytes.

LH An abbreviation for the Loadhigh command. *See* Loadhigh.

LIM EMS 4.0 The Lotus-Intel-Microsoft expanded memory specification, version 4.0, the most current version of LIM EMS. It allows up to 32 MB of expanded memory and allows for large chunks of mappable conventional memory to be swapped in and out of expanded memory. This is how some operating environments (such as DESQview) allow multitasking.

load high To load a device driver or memory-resident program into an upper memory block (UMB). *See also* Devicehigh, Loadhigh, upper memory blocks.

Loadhigh The MS-DOS command that loads a memory-resident program into an upper memory block. Loadhigh can be abbreviated as LH.

low-DOS memory Another term for conventional memory. *See* conventional memory.

megabyte (MB) Roughly 1 million bytes.

memory Circuitry that allows information to be stored and retrieved. There are two main types of memory: RAM and ROM. *See also* RAM, ROM.

memory-resident program A program that remains in memory even when it's not running so that it can be quickly activated for a specific task while another application is running. Memory-resident programs are also known as terminate-and-stay-resident programs (TSRs). One big drawback of memory-resident programs is that they are usually loaded into conventional memory, but MS-DOS allows them to be loaded into upper memory blocks. *See also* Loadhigh, upper memory blocks.

memory segment A 64-KB section of memory. The PC's basic 1-megabyte address space is divided into 65,536 segments. These segments are given values in hexadecimal, from 0000 through FFFF. In the Microsoft Diagnostics utility as well as with the Mem /m command, the memory segment at which a program has loaded is displayed.

microprocessor A central processing unit (CPU) on a single chip. *See also* '386, 80286, 8088/8086.

motherboard The main circuit board inside a computer. The motherboard usually contains the microprocessor, RAM, ROM, and expansion slots.

motherboard memory Memory that can be installed directly on a computer's motherboard. This term once referred only to conventional memory. However, 80286-based and '386-based computers can have both conventional and extended memory installed on their motherboards. On '386-based computers, motherboard memory is faster and more useful than memory added by means of an expansion card (with the exception of cards designed for special 32-bit memory expansion slots).

nanosecond One billionth of a second. The speed of RAM chips is measured in nanoseconds.

page A 16-KB bank of expanded memory.

page frame A 64-KB area in upper memory. Four 16-KB pages are mapped into the page frame by the expanded memory manager.

Pentium The next-generation microprocessor after the i486. This could be considered the "586" chip, although Intel decided to name the microprocessor Pentium for copyright purposes.

protected mode An operating mode of 80286 and '386 microprocessors that supports larger address spaces and more advanced features than real mode. Unfortunately, MS-DOS operates in real mode, which means that 80286 and '386 chips must run in real mode to run MS-DOS applications.

RAM Random Access Memory. Memory that can be read from or written to by the microprocessor.

RAM disk A simulated disk drive whose data is actually stored in RAM. A device driver, such as RAMDRIVE.SYS, can create a RAM disk in conventional, extended, or expanded memory. RAM disks are much faster than disk drives but have the disadvantage of losing their contents when the power goes off.

real mode An 80286 and '386 operating mode that is 8088/8086-compatible. In real mode, MS-DOS treats 80286 and '386 microprocessors as if they were very fast 8086 microprocessors.

reserved memory Another term for upper memory.

ROM Read-Only Memory. A type of memory that contains instructions or information the microprocessor can read but cannot change.

shadow RAM The process of copying the contents of a computer's ROM or BIOS into faster RAM. This improves the computer's overall speed but can cause memory conflicts.

SIMM Single In-line Memory Module. A bank of RAM chips, all installed on a tiny expansion card about half the size of a small comb.

SIP Single In-line Package. A type of housing for a collection of memory chips in which all the legs of the chips protrude from one side of the package.

SRAM Static Random Access Memory. A type of memory that is faster than DRAM, primarily because it doesn't need to be refreshed. SRAMs are used in some computers to speed operations. Their expense prevents them from being commonly used as main memory.

TSR Terminate-and-stay-resident. Another name for a memory-resident program. *See* memory-resident program.

UMBs *See* upper memory blocks.

upper memory The area of memory between 640 KB and 1 MB. That 384 KB of memory is used to store video memory, installable ROMs, and the ROM BIOS. Programs cannot run in upper memory, but you can load device drivers and memory-resident programs into UMBs using the Devicehigh and Loadhigh commands. *See also* Devicehigh, Loadhigh.

upper memory blocks Areas in upper memory not occupied by ROMs or video memory. The EMM386.EXE expanded memory emulator can map extended memory into these areas, creating upper memory blocks. MS-DOS needs a '386-based computer with extended memory for EMM386.EXE to do this. Device drivers and memory-resident programs can be loaded into UMBs with the Devicehigh and Loadhigh commands.

VCPI The Virtual Control Program Interface. This is a standard for writing MS-DOS programs that run in 80286 protected mode, 80386 protected mode, or 80386 virtual mode.

video memory Memory that stores the computer's display image.

wait state A pause that occurs when the microprocessor must wait for data from memory.

XMS *See* extended memory specification.

Appendix B

Command Summary

This appendix describes the commands that deal with memory and memory configuration. Elements that appear in square brackets ([ ]) are optional.

CONFIGURATION COMMANDS

Devicehigh

The Devicehigh command loads device drivers into UMBs.

```
devicehigh-[pathname]driver
```

pathname indicates the path to the device driver, complete with optional drive letter and subdirectories.

driver is the name of the device driver, followed by whatever switches and options the device driver requires.

To load the device driver into specific regions of upper memory, and to set the driver's size, use the following Devicehigh format:

```
devicehigh=[/L:region[,size1][;region2[,size2][/S]]] [pathname]driver
```

The /L switch directs MS-DOS to place the device driver into a specific region of upper memory.

region is a value ranging from 1 through 4 and representing a region of upper memory into which Devicehigh will load the device driver.

The *size1* value indicates the size of the device driver in memory: the amount of space, in bytes, required in a given region for the device driver. Devicehigh will attempt to load the device driver as best it can in the region specified.

region2 is a second region of upper memory for use by the device driver. It must be separated from the first region value by a semicolon. (Not all device drivers can load themselves into two regions; use the Mem /M command to determine if a device driver has the "split personality" necessary to load into two separate regions.)

size2 is the size of the device driver's second portion, loaded into another region of upper memory. Like *size1*, the value is in bytes.

The /S switch is used to shrink a device driver's UMB to its minimum size. This switch is primarily used by the MemMaker command.

Notes

- You must create UMBs with EMM386.EXE and the Dos command before you can use Devicehigh.

- If there isn't enough room for the device driver in upper memory, the device driver is loaded into conventional memory, as if the Device command had been used.

- The /L switch is usually set by the MemMaker utility. Devicehigh is smart enough on its own to load device drivers into upper memory. Only experts in memory management should consider messing with this switch.

- When using the /L switch, note that each PC has a different configuration. Some might have only one region in upper memory while others might have four. To determine how many regions your PC has, run the Microsoft Diagnostics utility and examine the upper memory map to check for different regions.

- The size option with the /L switch can be determined using the Mem /m command and naming the device driver already loaded into memory. Take a note of the driver's total size and then specify that value as size1 (or size2 if the driver can load into two separate regions).

Dos

The Dos command loads part of MS-DOS into the HMA and prepares MS-DOS for the UMBs created by EMM386.EXE.

```
dos=high¦low[,umb¦,noumb]
dos=[high,¦low,]umb¦noumb
```

The first option is either *high* or *low*. When *high* is specified, part of MS-DOS is loaded into the HMA; *low* (the default) places MS-DOS into conventional memory.

The second option is either *umb* or *noumb*. (If you use the first and second options together, they must be separated with a comma.) When *umb* is specified, MS-DOS prepares for the UMBs and allows you to use the Devicehigh and Loadhigh commands; *noumb* (the default) doesn't prepare MS-DOS for the UMBs. Devicehigh and Loadhigh cannot be used when *noumb* is specified.

Notes

- This command works only when HIMEM.SYS has been installed.

- The *umb* option works only on '386-based computers that have the EMM386.EXE device driver installed. Options must be separated with a comma.

- Consider specifying two Dos configuration commands if you're going to use both options. This allows you greater flexibility when performing a clean boot with the F8 key. (A clean boot prompts yes/ no for each command in CONFIG.SYS.)

EMM386.EXE

EMM386.EXE creates UMBs on '386-based computers with extended memory. EMM386.EXE can also simulate expanded memory by using extended memory on '386-based computers.

```
device=[pathname]emm386.exe [mode] [memory] [options] [noems ¦ ram]
```

pathname indicates the path to the EMM386.EXE device driver, complete with optional drive letter and subdirectories.

mode is either on, off, or auto. This turns the EMM386.EXE device driver's expanded memory support on or off or sets it to automatic. Setting mode to on enables expanded memory support. Setting mode to off disables expanded memory support. The default is on. Auto mode enables expanded memory support only when an application needs it.

memory indicates the amount (in kilobytes) of expanded memory to be simulated with extended memory. Values range from 64 (for 64 KB) through as much extended memory as is available. The maximum amount of simulated expanded memory is 32,768 (for 32 MB), and the default is zero (0 KB).

options represents the following options:

min=*size*   Specifies the minimum amount of EMS/VCPI memory EMM386.EXE will provide if that amount of memory is available. Values for *size* indicate kilobytes of expanded memory, and they range from 0 through the amount of memory specified by the *memory* option. If you specify the *noems* option, the default is zero.

w=on ¦ off   Turns support for the Weitek math coprocessor on or off.

m*x*   Gives the page frame address. The page frame address is controlled by *x* as shown:

1 = C000	8 = DC00
2 = C400	9 = E000
3 = C800	10 = 8000
4 = CC00	11 = 8400
5 = D000	12 = 8800
6 = D400	13 = 8C00
7 = D800	14 = 9000

frame=*address*   Also specifies the page frame address, although the *address* is one of the four-digit hex values listed above, instead of a code number.

/p*mmmm*   Also specifies the page frame address. *mmmm* is one of the four-digit hex values listed above.

p*n*=*address*   Specifies the exact locations of an EMS page. *n* indicates a page (a 16-KB chunk of memory), from 0 through 255. *address* is the memory location, identical to the values described for the three previous options.

x=*mmmm-nnnn*   Excludes a particular upper memory area from being used for a UMB. *mmmm* is the starting segment of the area, and *nnnn* is the ending segment of the area. This option takes priority over areas marked by the I option.

i=*mmmm-nnnn*   Includes a particular upper memory area for use as a UMB. *mmmm* is the starting segment of the area, and *nnnn* is the ending segment of the area.

b=*address*   Specifies a location in low memory, indicating the lowest address for EMS banking. Values for *address* are in the range of 1000 through 4000 hex, with 4000 hex as the default.

l=*minXMS*   Sets aside *minXMS* kilobytes of memory to be preserved as extended memory. The default value for *minXMS* is zero. (Notice that the option is the letter L, not the number 1.)

a=*altregs*   Specifies the number of fast alternate register sets (used for multitasking) you want to allocate to EMM386.EXE. Values for *altregs* range from 0 through 254, with 7 as the default. Every alternate register set adds about 200 bytes to the size in memory of EMM386.EXE.

h=*handles*   Specifies the number of EMS handles to use for accessing expanded memory. Values for *handles* range from 2 through 255, with 64 as the default.

d=*nnn*   Indicates the amount of memory needed for DMA buffering. Values for *nnn* are in kilobytes and range from 16 through 256, with 16 as the default.

ram[=*mmmm-nnnn*]   Specifies an upper memory area to be filled with RAM, creating UMBs. *mmmm* is the starting segment of the area, and *nnnn* is the ending segment of the area. If you use RAM by itself, EMM386 uses whatever upper memory areas are available to create UMBs.

noems   Creates UMBs without simulating any expanded memory with extended memory.

novcpi   Disables EMM386.EXE's VCPI support, but only when included with the noems option. Disabling VCPI support increases the amount of available extended memory.

highscan   Enables EMM386.EXE's "aggressive" scan of high memory. Don't use this option if your PC locks up or has problems running your applications.

/verbose   Directs EMM386.EXE to display status and error messages at startup. (This switch can be abbreviated as /v.)

win=*mmmm-nnnn*   Reserves an upper memory area for use by Windows instead of EMM386.EXE. *mmmm* is the starting segment of the area, and *nnnn* is the ending segment of the area.

nohi   Directs EMM386.EXE not to load part of itself into a UMB.

rom=*mmmm-nnnn*   Specifies an upper memory area that EMM386.EXE will use for shadow RAM. *mmmm* is the starting segment of the area, and *nnnn* is the ending segment of the area. Values for *mmmm* and *nnnn* range from A000 through FFFF hex.

nomovexbda   Prevents EMM386.EXE from moving the extended BIOS data from conventional memory to upper memory.

altboot   Specifies that EMM386.EXE is to use an alternate handler to reboot your computer when you press Ctrl+Alt+Del. Use this option only if your computer locks up or exhibits other unusual behavior when EMM386.EXE is loaded and you press Ctrl+Alt+Del.

Notes

■ Many of EMM386.EXE's options are for advanced users wishing to customize expanded memory performance on their PCs. The options you will use most frequently are *memory,* ram, noems, *x,* and *i.*

■ The HIMEM.SYS device driver must be installed before you install EMM386.EXE.

■ noems and ram cannot both be specified.

HIMEM.SYS

The HIMEM.SYS device driver establishes the XMS standard, manages extended memory in the computer, and allows MS-DOS to access the HMA.

```
device=[pathname]himem.sys [options]
```

pathname indicates the path to the HIMEM.SYS device driver, complete with optional drive letter and subdirectories.

options represents the following optional switches:

/a20control:on ¦ off   Specifies whether HIMEM.SYS will control the A20 line even if A20 was on when HIMEM.SYS was loaded. The default is on. If you specify off, HIMEM.SYS takes control of the A20 line only if A20 was off when HIMEM.SYS loaded.

/cpuclock:on ¦ off   Controls how HIMEM.SYS affects your PC's clock speed. The default setting is off. If you notice that your computer's speed changes when you load HIMEM.SYS, specify the on option.

/eisa   Directs HIMEM.SYS to control all of extended memory. This switch is required on EISA bus machines that have more than 16 MB of memory installed.

/hmamin=*m*   Specifies the amount of memory (in kilobytes) a program must use before HIMEM.SYS allows it to use the HMA. Values for *m* range from 0 through 63, with 0 as the default.

/int15=*xxx*   Provides access to extended memory for programs that use the old "Int 15h interface" instead of HIMEM.SYS's XMS method. Values for *xxx* indicate the number of kilobytes to provide, ranging from 64 through 65,535, with 0 as the default.

/numhandles=*n* Specifies the number of extended memory block handles that can be used simultaneously. Values for *n* range from 1 through 128, with 32 as the default. Each additional handle requires about 6 bytes of conventional memory.

/machine:*xxx*   Specifies what type of computer you are using. HIMEM usually detects what type of computer you are using, but there are a few computers HIMEM cannot detect. Values for *xxx* can be either a code or a number designating a particular computer type:

Code	Number	Computer Type
at	1	IBM PC/AT or compatible
ps2	2	IBM PS/2 system
ptlcascade	3	Phoenix Cascade BIOS
hpvectra	4	Hewlett-Packard Vectra PC (A and A+)
att6300plus	5	AT&T 6300 Plus PC
acer1100	6	The Acer 1100 PC
toshiba	7	Toshiba 1600 and 1200XE
wyse	8	Wyse 286 PC at 12.5 MHz
tulip	9	Tulip SX
zenith	10	Zenith ZBIOS machines
at1	11	IBM PC/AT (alternative delay)
at2	12	IBM PC/AT (alternative delay)
css	12	CSS Labs
at3	13	IBM PC/AT (alternative delay)
philips	13	Philips
fasthp	14	Hewlett-Packard Vectra
ibm7552	15	IBM 7552 Industrial Computer
bullmicral	16	Bull Micral 60
dell	17	Dell XBIOS PCs

/shadowram:on ┊ off   Specifies whether HIMEM.SYS should switch off shadow RAM. If your computer has less than 2 MB of memory, the default is off. Otherwise, the default is on.

/verbose   Directs HIMEM.SYS to display status and error messages at startup. (This switch can be abbreviated as /v.)

Notes

- HIMEM.SYS should be the first memory-management device driver installed in your CONFIG.SYS file. (Only hard-disk device drivers should come before it.)

- Normally, none of HIMEM.SYS's switches or options need to be specified.

RAMDRIVE.SYS

The RAMDRIVE.SYS device driver creates a RAM disk in either conventional, extended, or expanded memory.

`device=[pathname]ramdrive.sys [size [sector [entries]]] [/E|/A]`

pathname indicates the path to the RAMDRIVE.SYS device driver, complete with optional drive letter and subdirectories.

size is the size of the RAM disk in kilobytes. Values for *size* range from 4 through 32,767, for a 4-KB through 32-MB RAM disk. When *size* isn't specified, a 64-KB RAM disk is created.

sector is the size of the RAM disk's sectors in bytes. Large sector sizes are good for large files, and small sector sizes are good for small files. Values for *sector* can be 128, 256, or 512, with 512 as the default. If you specify a sector size, you must also include the size of the RAM disk.

entries indicates the number of directory entries (places where MS-DOS stores filenames) that RAMDRIVE.SYS will create in the RAM disk's root directory. Values for *entries* range from 2 through 1024, with 64 as the default. If you specify the number of entries, you must also specify a sector size and the size of the RAM disk.

/E or /A directs RAMDRIVE.SYS to create the RAM disk in extended or expanded memory. If both switches are omitted, the RAM disk is created in conventional memory.

Notes

- You must have enough memory to create the RAM disk. If you don't have enough memory to create a RAM disk of the specified size, RAMDRIVE.SYS creates a smaller RAM disk.

- When the *sector* or *entries* option is specified, you must also specify all parameters that precede it.

- Each RAM disk created is given the next-highest available drive letter in your computer.

MS-DOS COMMANDS

Emm386

EMM386.EXE is both a device driver and an MS-DOS command for '386-based computers. As a command, it displays the current status of the EMS driver and turns expanded memory support on or off.

```
emm386 [on¦off¦auto] [w=on¦w=off]
```

When used without any options, the Emm386 command displays the status of expanded memory support in your system.

The first option is either on, off, or auto. The on option turns the EMM386.EXE device driver on, off turns it off, and auto activates auto mode. In auto mode, expanded memory support is enabled only when an application needs it. The default is on.

The second option is either w=on or w=off and is used to activate support for a Weitek math coprocessor. The default is w=off.

Notes

You cannot turn off expanded memory support when UMBs have been created.

Loadhigh

The Loadhigh command loads memory-resident programs into UMBs. It is an internal MS-DOS command and can be abbreviated *lh*.

```
loadhigh [pathname]filename
```

pathname is the path to the memory-resident program, complete with optional drive letter and subdirectories.

filename is the name of a memory-resident program. The filename is followed by the switches or options that would typically follow it on the command line or in a batch file.

To load memory-resident programs into specific regions of upper memory, and to set the program's size, Loadhigh takes on the following format:

```
loadhigh [/L:region[,size1][;region2[,size2]][/S]] [pathname]filename
```

The /L switch directs MS-DOS to load the memory-resident program into a specific region of upper memory.

region indicates a region of upper memory into which the memory-resident program will be loaded. It's a value ranging from 1 through 4, depending on the number of regions of upper memory in your PC.

size1 is the memory-resident program's resident size in bytes. This value is optional; Loadhigh attempts to load the memory-resident program as best it can in the specified region.

region2 is optional. It indicates a second region of upper memory for use by memory-resident programs that might split themselves into two parts. The value must be separated from the first region value by a semicolon. (Use the Mem /m command to determine if a memory-resident program loads in two separate pieces.)

size2 is the size of the second portion of a memory-resident program that can split into two parts. The value is in bytes.

The /S switch is by the MemMaker command to shrink a UMB to its minimum size while a memory-resident program is loading.

Notes

- You must create UMBs with EMM386.EXE and the Dos command before you can use Loadhigh.

- If there isn't enough room in upper memory, the memory-resident program is loaded into conventional memory.

- The /L switch is primarily for use by the MemMaker utility. Loadhigh is more than capable of loading your memory-resident programs high without the /L switch.

- To determine how many regions of upper memory your PC has, run the Microsoft Diagnostics utility and examine the upper memory map.

- Use the Mem /m command, followed by the name of a memory-resident program, to obtain the program's size for use with the /L switch's *size* option. The bottom line of output from the Mem /m command will tell you the memory-resident program's total size.

Mem

The Mem command reports on the status of your computer's used and free memory and, optionally, the contents of memory.

```
mem [/classify ¦ /debug ¦ /free ¦ /module name] [/page]
```

When used without switches, the Mem command provides a summary of the free and used conventional, upper, expanded, and extended memories in your system.

The Mem command's first four optional switches are /classify, /debug, /free, and /module, which can be abbreviated /C, /D, /F, and /M. Only one of these switches can be specified at a time.

/classify displays a summary of all loaded device drivers and memory-resident programs and indicates whether they're in the conventional or the upper memory area. A detailed memory summary ends the listing.

/debug displays a detailed listing of the entire contents of MS-DOS memory, including resident MS-DOS device drivers and low-level information.

/free displays a summary of available conventional and upper memory.

/module provides detailed information on a specific device driver or memory-resident program in memory. *name* is the name of the device driver or memory-resident program, minus the extension (SYS, EXE, and so on). The Mem command describes the location of the device driver or memory-resident program in memory and gives its total size.

/page pauses the Mem command's output after each screen of text. This works in the same way as the Dir command's /P switch. (/page can also be abbreviated as /P.)

Notes

The MS-DOS 5 Mem command's /program switch is no longer available in MS-DOS version 6. Use the /debug switch instead.

MemMaker

The MemMaker utility optimizes your computer's memory by loading device drivers and memory-resident programs into upper memory. To do this, MemMaker examines your PC's memory configuration and customizes the way your device drivers and memory-resident programs are loaded high. MemMaker makes the job of memory management a snap, and it can often load more device drivers and memory-resident programs high than you can manually.

```
memmaker [/b] [/batch] [/session] [/swap:drive] [/t] [/undo] [w:n,m]
```

By itself, the MemMaker command will evaluate memory and scan CON-FIG.SYS and AUTOEXEC.BAT. It's an interactive program, allowing you to select options and make decisions. During the MemMaker process, your computer will reboot more than once.

The /b switch runs MemMaker in black and white.

The /batch switch runs MemMaker in the unattended mode. The default options will be selected, and McmMaker will proceed through all of its operations without any user input. (''Batch'' here has nothing to do with the MS-DOS batch programming language.)

The /session switch is used exclusively by MemMaker during optimization.

The /swap switch alerts MemMaker to the presence of a compressed hard drive, one created with DoubleDisk, Stacker, or a similar program. If the compressed drive is drive C, the new drive letter of the original drive C (that boots your PC) must be specified after /swap and a colon. (When you install a disk-doubling program such as Stacker, the program divides your hard disk into two areas: a compressed area and an uncompressed area. These areas function as separate hard disks. As your computer boots, the compressed area is assigned the drive letter C, and the uncompressed area is assigned the next available drive letter.) For example:

```
/swap:d
```

It's assumed that the drive letter D is assigned to the original or ''host'' (uncompressed) drive.

The /t switch disables detection of IBM Token-Ring networks. Use this switch if your computer uses such a network and you're having problems running MemMaker.

The /undo switch pulls out all of MemMaker's most recent modifications to CONFIG.SYS and AUTOEXEC.BAT.

The /W switch reserves portions of upper memory for use by Microsoft Windows. The two options, *n* and *m,* set aside two portions of upper memory for use by Windows, usually 12 KB each. If you're not using Windows, you can specify zero for both *n* and *m* to make as much as 24 KB of upper memory available to other programs.

Notes

- MemMaker uses the SIZER.EXE program and CHKSTATE.SYS device driver, both of which are found in your MS-DOS directory. Do not delete these files from disk!

- MEMMAKER.INF is a text file that can be edited to instruct the MemMaker utility to ignore or REM out specific device drivers, memory-resident programs, or other programs that might be found in CONFIG.SYS or AUTOEXEC.BAT. Refer to the instructions at the start of MEMMAKER.INF before editing this file.

- Refer to Chapter 6 for information on running MemMaker.

SMARTDRV

SMARTDrive creates a disk cache in your computer by using extended memory.

```
smartdrv [[drive[+¦-]]...] [options]
```

Without any options, SMARTDrive will read-cache all floppy drives and both read- and write-cache your hard disks. SMARTDrive ignores RAM drives, CD-ROM drives, compressed drives, ''flash-memory card'' drives, and network drives. Drives created using the InterLink program are read-cached.

The size of the cache SMARTDrive automatically creates depends on the total amount of memory in your PC:

Extended memory	Cache size	Cache in Windows
Up to 1 MB	All extended memory	0 KB
Up to 2 MB	1 MB	256 KB
Up to 4 MB	1 MB	512 KB
Up to 6 MB	2 MB	1 MB
6 MB or more	2 MB	2 MB

When Windows is running, it reduces the cache size to make more extended memory available. The two values, the MS-DOS cache size and the Windows cache size, can be adjusted using SMARTDrive's *max* and *min* options (discussed below).

drive is a disk drive letter, minus the colon. A drive letter alone directs SMARTDrive to read-cache the drive. A plus sign following the drive letter enables both read- and write-caching for the drive. A minus sign following the drive disables all caching for that drive.

options include the following switches and optional parameters:

/e:*elementsize*   Sets the size of the memory chunks SMARTDrive moves when reading from and writing to disk. Values for *elementsize* are in bytes 1024, 2048, 4096, and the default value of 8192. The larger the *elementsize* value, the more conventional memory SMARTDrive uses.

max   Specifies the maximum size for the disk cache in kilobytes. The default is determined by the above table.

min   Specifies the size for the cache when Windows runs. Windows reduces the cache size to *min* kilobytes to make more extended memory available. When Windows quits, the cache size is restored to the value specified by *max*. This value must be specified after *max*.

/b:*buffersize*   Sets the size of SMARTDrive's read-ahead buffer in kilobytes. (A read-ahead buffer is additional information that SMARTDrive reads when an application reads information from disk.) The value must be a multiple of the value specified after the /E switch, with a default size of 16 KB.

/C   Clears the cache, writing all information stored in the write-ahead buffer to disk. (Normally the information is only written after a period of inactivity or when the write-ahead buffer is full.)

/R   Restarts SMARTDrive, writing whatever data is in the write-ahead buffer to disk and clearing the read-ahead buffer.

/L   Directs SMARTDrive to load into conventional memory regardless of the presence of UMBs. Without this switch, SMARTDrive will attempt to load itself into a UMB.

/Q   Runs SMARTDrive in the "quiet" mode; no information will be displayed on the screen when SMARTDrive initially loads.

/verbose   Directs SMARTDRV.SYS to display status and error messages at startup. (This switch can be abbreviated as /v.)

/S   Displays extra statistics about SMARTDrive's operation, the number of cache hits and misses.

In CONFIG.SYS, SMARTDrive might appear in the following format:

```
device=c:\dos\smartdrv.exe /double_buffer
```

The /double_buffer switch is required by some hard disks when EMM386.EXE is used with SMARTDrive, or to run Windows in the enhanced mode. Refer to the section in Chapter 7 titled "SMARTDrive's Double Buffering Option" for additional information.

Notes

■ SMARTDrive is automatically loaded high, providing there is room for it in a UMB. There is no need to insert the Loadhigh command in front of the command that loads SMARTDRV.EXE.

■ Always type *smartdrv* /c before rebooting your computer. If your system has a SHUTDOWN.BAT file, specify this command on the last line of the batch file to ensure that any information in the write-ahead buffer is written to disk before you shut down.

■ To prevent Windows from reducing the size of the disk cache, specify the same value for both *min* and *max*.

■ Starting with MS-DOS version 6, SMARTDrive is a memory-resident program loaded in AUTOEXEC.BAT. Note that SMARTDrive no longer can use expanded memory and, by the same token, the /A switch used by previous versions of SMARTDrive is no longer present.

Index

Italicized page numbers refer to illustrations.

Special Characters

- (Debug prompt), 33
? (Debug help command), 33
~ (tilde), 135
386 enhanced mode (Windows), 30, 123,
    124, 126, 152
386MAX software
    installing and optimizing, 140–44,
        150–51, 160
    overview, 137–38, 163
    using video memory, 153–55
486SX and i486DX2 microprocessors, 9, 13
586 microprocessors. *See* Pentium
    microprocessor
8088 and 8086 microprocessors. *See*
    computers, 8088/8086-based
80286 microprocessors. *See* computers,
    80286-based
80386SX and 80386DX microprocessors.
    See computers, 80386-based

A

A20 handlers, 73
access time, 11
address bus, 7–9
addresses, memory, 6, 34–35, 179
address space, 8, 179
ANSI.SYS, 88–89, *89,* 90–92, *93,* 132
Append program (MS-DOS), 133
applications. *See* programs; software
AUTOEXEC.BAT. *See also* setup
    scenarios
    booting interactively, 102
    creating disk caches, 117–19
    creating RAM disks, 111, 112–14
    moving memory-resident programs into
        UMBs, 95–98
    strategy for modifying, 70–71, 84

AUTOEXEC.BAT, *continued*
    for third-party memory managers,
        140–42, 145, 146, 148, 149–50,
        159–62
    Windows, 125, 134, 136

B

backfill memory, 21–22, 60, 61, 179
banks of memory, 10, 48, 53
bank-switched memory, 19
Basic Input/Output System. *See* BIOS
batch files, 111, 114–15
binary numbers, 5–6
BIOS, 17, 35, 102, 180
bits, 5–6, 7, 8, 14, 180
BlueMAX, 138. *See also* 386MAX
    software
booting
    creating Startup Disk, 70–71
    interactive, 77, 94
buffers
    disk, 157
    print, 25, 121
buses, 4
bytes, 6, 14, 180

C

cache memory, 12–13
caches, disk. *See also* SMARTDRV.EXE
    386MAX software, 138
    creating, 117–19
    Fastopen command versus, 119
    overview, 116–20, 122, 180
    Windows, 125, 128–29, 136
CGA video memory. *See* video memory
Chkdsk command, 108–9, 120, 135
clock cycles, 11
clusters, 120, 135

DAN GOOKIN

Dan Gookin indites treatises unpretentious on subjects heterogeneous, obviating complexity in a modus risibilis. With absorbing parlance he slices the Gordian knot of computerese, replanting it with unobjectionable, elucidative, and comprehendible banter. And he makes it easy to read, too.

The manuscript for this book was prepared and submitted to Microsoft Press in electronic form. Text files were processed and formatted using Microsoft Word.

Principal editorial compositor: Barb Runyan
Principal typographer: Lisa Iversen
Systems technician: Carol L. Luke
Interior text designer: Kim Eggleston
Principal illustrator: Lisa Sandburg
Cover designer: Rebecca Geisler
Cover illustrator: Henk Dawson
Cover color separator: Walker Graphics
Indexer: Matthew Spence

Text composition by Microsoft Press in Garamond Light with display type in Futura Heavy, using the Magna composition system. Composed pages were delivered to the printer as electronic prepress files.

Printed on recycled paper stock.

Push Your PC to the Max!

MS-DOS® to the Max
Using the MS-DOS 6 Tools to
Make Your Hard Disk Scream

Dan Gookin

With Dan Gookin's help and humor, you can boost your performance, safeguard your data, and create the ultimate MS-DOS–based system. Exploit the new features of version 6 of the MS-DOS operating system to the fullest with more than 40 disk-based batch files, utilities, and programs—tools that will tap your system's power potential! In this book you'll find easy-to-use strategies, subtle tricks, and handy shortcuts that will help you:

- use little-known CONFIG.SYS and AUTOEXEC.BAT techniques to personalize your PC and manage multiple configurations

- apply time-proven techniques and new commands to organize your hard disk and manage your files

- take advantage of the new MS-DOS power tools

- unravel the mystery of buying a new drive for your system and learn how to configure once and for all

- and much more!

The accompanying disk includes all of the batch files and debug scripts in the book; plus two configuration "Wizards" and several bonus tools that will push your system *to the Max.*

352 pages, softcover with one 3.5-inch disk $29.95 ($39.95 Canada)   ISBN 1-55615-548-4
Available April 1993
